Open Door on John

A Gospel for Our Time

Phillip McFadyen

TRIANGLE

First Published in Great Britain in 1998
Triangle
SPCK, Holy Trinity Church
Marylebone Road
London NW1 4DU

Bible passages beginning each section are from the *New International Version* © 1973, 1978, 1984 by the International Bible Society. Used by permission of Hodder & Stoughton Limited.

Bible quotations used in the text are from the Revised Standard Version © 1971 and 1955.

British Library Cataloguing-in-Publication Data
A catalogue record of this book is available from the British Library

ISBN 0-281-05147-X

Typeset by David Benham, Norwich, Norfolk
Printed in Great Britain by The Cromwell Press, Melksham, Wiltshire

Contents

Foreword

It is a privilege to commend this introduction to the Fourth Gospel. The author has succeeded in making more accessible the mysteries and compelling figure of Jesus Christ. We need help to understand his narrative, which asserts that He is the Way, the Truth, the Life, the Word, the Door, the Bread of Life and the Resurrection.

An honest reading today finds difficulties; we are likely to approach in the spirit in which we listen to BBC Radio 4's 'Today Programme'. Is this literally true? Who wrote this? Was he there? Are not some of the claims made by Christ about Himself psychologically extraordinary? Are not some of the comments on 'the Jews' impossible for us who all live post-Auschwitz? Is this poetry or history?

This brief guide is designed both for personal meditation and for groups slowly to examine some of the stumbling blocks to our appreciation of St John. After a lively treatment of each chapter revealing our author's attractive and learned enthusiasm, two principal characters are quizzed . . . Did Mary Magdalene think she was being stereotyped? Had she something to say on women's issues? Who is the enigmatic 'beloved disciple'? Is he a role model for today's followers of Jesus?

To be accessible and welcoming with the door open has long been the not uncostly character of Ranworth Church, Vicarage, village and Broad. The tower's panoramic views, the screen with its angels, women saints and white roses, and the Antiphoner tracing the year's music, the Church all bathed in Norfolk sunlight, hint at an extraordinary past that lives today in fresh initiatives. The coach house is now a Visitors' Centre with art exhibitions (though there is still a horse in the paddock). Here in Ranworth Church thanksgiving for women newly ordained seemed to foreshadow freshly inspired worship. Contemporary thinking on belief is a hallmark of this community from which this commentary has been born.

Symbol and sign, sacrament and mystery, all found in the life lived in Palestine 2000 years ago, are the ways to Eternity chosen by this spiritual gospel. This way has never been more memorably proclaimed than in Shelley's lines:

Heaven's light for ever shines, Earth's shadows fly;
Life, like a dome of many-coloured glass,
Stains, the white radiance of Eternity . . .

One of the doors of the spirit for all seekers in the Gospel of St. John.

Alan Webster
Formerly Dean of St Paul's

Preface

Why another commentary on John's Gospel? After all, there are enough to choose from. One might cynically quote John himself and say, 'I suppose that the world itself could not contain the books that could be written' (21.25). So why another book? The reason for writing this one is to bridge the gap between theological scholarship and the searching lay person who simply wants to be treated seriously but not patronized when he or she enquires what this Gospel is about.

John's Gospel above all others is for the seeking enquirer. The person who wants to 'come and see' what all this is about. Many of the characters in this Gospel are driven by this same urge. Andrew, Nathanael, the woman at the well and many others come with questions and are astounded by the response they get. All are taken seriously and treated with respect. Of course they are all characters who have been given life by the writing of this amazing storyteller whom we call the evangelist John. It is my belief that the writer of this Gospel had a driving ambition to relate his story to those who would listen. Like some 'ancient mariner' he holds us with his 'glittering eye'. This is a story for the perceptive, those who are willing to see beyond the immediate and to glimpse 'heaven in ordinarie' as George Herbert once described the quest for prayer.

Once universally known as the 'spiritual Gospel', John would be better understood as the Gospel for our time. It concerns itself with life in all its fullness and challenges us to look into an open heaven. The 'doors of perception' as described by Aldous Huxley in the late 1950s are not nudged open by a drug-induced state but rather by a clear vision of the one to whom this Gospel testifies. Who Jesus is and what he represents is the subject of these pages. For too long too many people have stood with the Christ in Holman Hunt's painting of 'The Light of the World' knocking at the door. These notes are offered as a manual to enable that door to be opened, at least for those who want a glimpse of the open heaven that this Gospel describes.

I would like to thank all those who generously helped me with this manuscript. It was written while I was recovering from an operation which made typing difficult. There were a number of kind people who typed to my dictation and others who encouraged me to persevere when the going was tough. My thanks to my wife and family for their long-suffering and patience. I am grateful to David Benham for coming to the rescue when the computer got the better of me and to John Nicolls, who read the text and made perceptive comments. Finally thanks to my parish who have been ever ready to allow me to share these thoughts with them through sermons and Bible study.

Phillip McFadyen

Phillip McFadyen was born in 1944 and went to school in Liverpool. At fifteen he entered art school, studying Book Illustration and qualifying as an art teacher. He read Theology at King's College, London, and did some post graduate work in New Testament studies. He trained for the ministry at St Augustine's College, Canterbury.

He is the author of *Open Door on Luke* (Benham, 1995), *Open Door on Mark* (SPCK, 1996) and Corinthian Columns (Canterbury Press, 1997).

He was ordained in Sheffield and was curate of St Mark's, Broomhill for three years. He then became chaplain and lecturer at Keswick Hall College of Education. After 23 years in The Norwich Diocese he is now Vicar at Ranworth with Panxworth and Woodbastwick, as well as Clergy Training Officer and honorary canon of Norwich Cathedral.

His enthusiasm is for:

opening minds to understand the scriptures. Luke 24.45

Introduction

The Gospel of John has a fascination for many people. What was the writer's intention, why is his material so different? The writers of the first three Gospels can be compared to painters in a life class. They view the model differently. Each has his own style, his own composition and his own particular emphasis. Mark is in a hurry to capture the main points. His short vivid brushstrokes evoke an immediate response and encourage the viewer to get involved with the subject. Matthew at first appears to be a derivative painter. He has a respect for the old masters even though his style is one of confrontation. There is a dreamlike quality to his work, especially in the opening chapters, which makes connections with other schools of painting; the work is so well organized that it is easy to access. Luke's painting has a patrician air, but it is also full of social comment. His work is also derivative and dependent on other sources, but there is a narrative quality in the portrait that immediately engages those who are looking for a more universal theme. If John were also to be admitted to this class we might be surprised to find that he spent a long time in contemplating the subject without actually touching his canvas. He is more likely to make a few preliminary studies in his sketch book and complete the painting many years later.

John, of all the Gospels, should be treated like wine. It can improve by being laid down in the subconscious to mellow and mature. That is not too surprising if we come to understand the work as having evolved slowly. In the business of New Testament studies, we have more to learn from poets than scholars. The Gospels should be regarded as great literary works as well as theological source documents. We tend to forget that sacred Scripture has more to do with creative artistry than accountancy or science. Perhaps John is better appreciated by those with a deep love and respect for his artistry than those too keen to dissect his work for the history behind it. How sad it would be if students of Shakespeare were only concerned with unearthing the text of Hollinshed behind Macbeth and quite forgot to look at the play and its meaning. We shall try to keep this issue in front of us as we study this Gospel. It is well to remember that for the poet Browning the study of John brought 'new significance and fresh result', for:

What first were guessed as points, I now knew to be stars.

The popularity of this Gospel is well attested. Each time I have asked people which eight books of the Bible they would like to take with them on a desert island they invariably choose John as a prime candidate. John is even favoured above Acts, which might be a more practical choice, containing, as it does, advice on travelling and how to survive shipwreck! However, even if John is most people's favourite Gospel, it is probably the least understood. It begins with a philosophical treatise on the 'Word' and ends with a fishing trip. In between there are signs and sayings which have puzzled readers for centuries. Stones are not turned into bread but water is changed into wine by the gallon. There is no description of the institution of the eucharist, yet Jesus talks of himself as the bread of life. He weeps for his friend Lazarus but not over Jerusalem. He cleanses the temple at the beginning of his ministry and quickly gets into an argument with the authorities, who conspire to destroy him. To some this Gospel appears to be fiercely anti-Semitic, and yet it commands a gospel of love (15.17). There is no love or understanding shown for Judas even though he is necessary to the scheme of things which delivers up Jesus to be crucified. In contrast, there is an unnamed 'beloved disciple' who is favoured in the text above Peter and may be the inspiration behind the authorship of this Gospel.

The Jesus presented in this Gospel is an enigma. He invites followers to 'come and see' who he is, and yet he plays a game of 'hide and seek'. He promises an open heaven to those who can perceive it and believe in him. The prologue identifies him with the pre-existent 'Word' present with God at the creation. He talks of himself in language usually associated with the Godhead, and yet speaks of the Father as being greater. He dies in agony and shame on a cross, committing his mother to the care of his beloved disciple; and when he rises from the dead he is mistaken for a gardener by a woman who is commissioned to be the first apostle. At every turn in the narrative he is both elusive and charismatic. The reader is left in no doubt that those who 'see' Jesus have in some mysterious sense seen the Father.

So different is John that scholars are undecided as to his relationship with the other Gospel writers. No one can be certain if the author was familiar with the other evangelists' work or the tradition behind them. The writer sprinkles clues and hints which have tantalized his readers into thinking he may or may not know the material. In fact John makes a number of oblique references which leave this question unresolved.

The picture of Jesus is also very different. The text is littered with hints and revelations as to who Jesus is and how he relates to the Father. The writer is deeply concerned to open a door onto the nature and meaning of Jesus as the revealer of God in the world. We can only speculate what prompted such an overriding concern. John tells us at the end of chapter 20 that he has written his testimony so that those who read it might believe that Jesus is the 'Christ, the Son of God', and that believing, the reader may have life. He has recalled this information for this sole purpose. He has made a careful selection of what he calls 'signs' which, he claims, Jesus performed. These signs are the key to opening the doors of perception for the believer. By recalling these events John is not simply telling us what happened as a matter of history, he is concerned to draw out the significance of the events after a great deal of reflection. The process is akin to that of falling in love. When people fall in love their attitude to life changes, they become vulnerable, they are prepared to take risks and most of all their perceptions are heightened. In recalling the story of Jesus, John invites his readers to embark on a trusting, loving relationship with Jesus of Nazareth. Those who are prepared to take such risks and 'attend' to the Jesus of this Gospel will receive power to become the children of God (1.12). They will become one with their beloved. This is the prayer of Jesus in chapter 17 that he and his disciples should become one (vv. 11, 21, 23). The believer is united with Jesus in and through the recognition of the 'signs'. John only classifies two of the miracles as 'signs'. Various commentators have indicated others. Readers will produce their own list, but generally, most agree to there being seven; six taking place before the crucifixion and the seventh being the crucifixion itself. As with most things in this Gospel, however, there are different ways of viewing the signs. For instance, the crucifixion can be seen simply as the death of a man or as the final victory of God over the forces of evil. By recognizing and interpreting the signs in John, the disciple discerns the activity of God at work in the person of Jesus. God's love for his world is demonstrated in the sacrificial self-giving of Jesus. In dying on the cross, Jesus is seen to be the ultimate pointer to God. He is literally 'lifted up' on a sign post, hoisted up as a signal as the perfect icon of God's love for the world. Once this is seen the disciple becomes irresistibly drawn and incorporated in the love that the Son shares with the Father. In seeing Jesus like this the reader is left in no doubt that he has encountered the Father.

This Gospel is primarily concerned with painting a picture of Jesus in which we see the work and activity of God. The 'Word' which activated the creative process is accessible in the person and ministry of Jesus Christ. The inevitable question arises as to how much of this is true. 'What is truth?' asks Pilate of Jesus, but John gives us an answer at the beginning of his Gospel. The Word made flesh is seen to be 'full of grace and truth' (1.14), it supersedes that which came through Moses and it makes God known. This is John's overriding concern. It is his only reason for writing, and all his gifts of storytelling and dialogue are focused on this one goal. His portrait of Jesus is coloured by this perspective throughout.

As John sees it, the good news is that God has revealed himself in Jesus Christ. He has become enfleshed in a real person so that we can become real people. Real people experience life in all its fullness – that is the promise that Jesus makes in this Gospel. Life is available to those who can open the door and see beyond the mundane and material. As George Herbert says:

A man that looks on glass
on it may stay his eye;
or if he pleaseth, through it pass
and then the heaven espy.

The reader of this Gospel may take things at face value or look through and beyond the glass into the open heaven towards which the Gospel points.

There are a number of characters in this Gospel who face this challenge. Some have their eyes opened, others choose to stay their eye on the glass. At the end of this book, I shall ask two of them what they thought of Jesus and why they think John made use of their story. Through this imaginary discussion, we can try to understand the role they play in unravelling the mystery of Jesus.

So if the Jesus of John seems to walk taller than the Jesus of the other Gospels, if his discourses seem to be stately monologues and if he seems too self-assured and on another plane, we need not necessarily conclude that the historical Jesus would have behaved exactly like this. John is engaged with the significance of these events rather than simply recording history. He tells us *what is going on* rather than *what took place*. History is secondary to meaning. Truth is a matter of God-given insight. It is to do with the acceptance of Jesus as the incarnate Word of God, and it is experienced in attending to the Jesus of this Gospel. Once this is accepted then the Gospel makes more sense. It is telling us who Jesus is and how faith in him can radically change lives.

PALESTINE
in the time of JESUS

How to Use this Book

Many people are afraid to embark on a course of Bible study. They think it is reserved either for the professional theologian or for the naturally pious. Neither of these assumptions is true. Bible study is for anyone willing to get involved with the text. Those who like to wrestle like Jacob with the angel in the Old Testament will come out of the experience better and wiser if not a little bruised by the encounter.

This Gospel, above all, is the most feared by the enquiring seeker. Somehow it seems more mysterious, more holy than the others, better treated with more respect and kept at a safe distance. That should not be the case. John wants the reader to benefit from this Gospel. It is written with the purpose of bringing the reader to a knowledge of eternal life. That understanding does not come without getting to grips with this text. This book is meant to encourage the faint-hearted to have a go and probe a little more deeply by asking a few pertinent questions. The answers are not provided, but a discussion might enable a fuller understanding.

In order to facilitate discussion, the commentary has been arranged into a seven-week course of weekday studies. The final week, seven, has two extra days to take the reader into the weekend in order to complete the course with the resurrection appearances. The course could usefully be employed as a basis for a Lent study group, but will need to start before Ash Wednesday in order to complete by Easter Day.

Working with a Group

This book is designed to be used in groups. It is meant to encourage discussion and debate. If you engage in this method you need to have some clear aims.

First, stick to the text of John. People are easily diverted into general discussion about the state of the Church and about morality, and are even happy to give their prejudices an airing. John's Gospel is the perfect antidote to this. Jesus, in this Gospel, is single-minded, and we should be also.

Give everyone a chance to participate. Look for the naturally reticent and invite them to comment or tell their story. Remember how Jesus does this with the woman at the well (4.4–26). Such people often have the brightest pearls, but their shell needs opening.

It will help to keep your group focused to have some clear questions to set before them. Have some answers in mind, but try to encourage them to formulate their own response. For instance:

A) Why was John written?
   To answer the questions: 'Who is Jesus?' 'What does he stand for?'
B) For whom was this Gospel written?
   For those who want to follow Jesus – his disciples.
C) What does the Gospel of John say?
   In order to be a disciple you need to follow Jesus through suffering to glory.

Ice-breakers

Openness is the theme: being open to the good news as John presents it, being open to one another as we discover what discipleship means. To achieve this, it might help for your group to get to know each other better. This will enable them to participate more fully. If Bible study is to be fun and enjoyable, then you want everyone to get involved as soon as possible. Here are some suggestions.

1) Listening Exercise. Number the members of the group one-two-three, one-two-three, one-two-three. Ask 'number ones' to tell 'number twos' who they are, where they are from and what they enjoy doing. 'Number two' then introduces 'number one' to 'number three' and they then compare notes. This is a good exercise in listening, especially for the 'number twos'.
2) Buzz groups. Divide the group into threes and compile a list of favourite stories from John. This will encourage familiarity with the Gospel and whet appetites for the study.

These exercises are not necessary but might encourage your group to gel if they do not know each other. They should take no more than ten minutes at the most.

How to Organize the Bible Study

First you need to decide how long you have and how much ground you intend to cover.

Studying One Section

First, set aside an hour to familiarize the group with a whole section, for example, Section 3, 'Things Happen'.

- Arrange your group in a circle.
- Allocate twelve minutes for each 'day reading'. (There are five to each section.)
- Invite members to read aloud, in turn, through the first reading, for example, 'A Free Lunch for 5,000' (John 6.1–15). This should take two to three minutes.
- The leader then either reads out the commentary or summarizes it.
- Divide the people into 'buzz groups' of three members each and ask them to consider one of the questions listed in connection with the passage.
- Stop the discussion after five minutes.
- Repeat this procedure for the remaining readings of the section.

If you keep to the suggested timing, this should take only one hour and will stimulate your group to study John's Gospel further. The whole process will be facilitated by asking your group to read through the material before the meeting.

If this is a successful procedure, and your group wants to do more, you might arrange a monthly ongoing Bible study to cover the whole Gospel in seven months, or seven weeks if you meet weekly.

Studying One Reading

This will look at one reading of the section in more detail, for example, 'Mary Sees the Lord' (John 20.1–18). Again, allow at least one hour for this exercise.

- Arrange seating in a circle.
- Emphasize the context by referring to the section title, 'Jesus Is Lifted Up'. This will help the group understand John's theme better.
- The leader reads out the commentary and invites others to make their observations. Do they agree, or disagree? Are they challenged? Have they anything they want to add? What does the passage say to them about openness? How does it apply to their church situations?
- Divide the people into smaller groups to tackle the set questions, perhaps allocating different questions to different groups, or all tackling the questions together, depending upon the time available.
- Draw together the discussion by inviting comments and insights to be shared in the final plenary session.

Obviously this method is going to be more demanding on time, especially if the group if committed to an ongoing study of the whole Gospel. This needs to be discussed with the group.

One possible solution is to combine both methods in a two-hour Bible study. One reading can be chosen to be studied in more depth in the second hour, while the whole section is given the first treatment in the first hour. Remember, whatever you do, keep to the text and help everybody enjoy the challenge.

AN OPENING IS MADE

Begin at the beginning

John 1.1–18

¹**In the beginning was the Word, and the Word was with God, and the Word was God.** ²He was with God in the beginning. ³Through him all things were made; without him nothing was made that has been made. ⁴In him was life, and that life was the light of men. ⁵The light shines in the darkness, but the darkness has not understood it.

⁶There came a man who was sent from God; his name was John. ⁷He came as a witness to testify concerning that light, so that through him all men might believe. ⁸He himself was not the light; he came only as a witness to the light. ⁹The true light that gives light to every man was coming into the world.

¹⁰He was in the world, and though the world was made through him, the world did not recognise him. ¹¹He came to that which was his own, but his own did not receive him. ¹²Yet to all who received him, to those who believed in his name, he gave the right to become children of God — ¹³children born not of natural descent, nor of human decision or a husband's will, but born of God.

¹⁴The Word became flesh and made his dwelling among us. We have seen his glory, the glory of the One and Only, who came from the Father, full of grace and truth. ¹⁵John testifies concerning him. He cries out, saying, 'This was he of whom I said, "He who comes after me has surpassed me because he was before me."' ¹⁶From the fulness of his grace we have all received one blessing after another. ¹⁷For the law was given through Moses; grace and truth came through Jesus Christ. ¹⁸No-one has ever seen God, but God the One and Only, who is at the Father's side, has made him known.

By beginning at the beginning as he does, John opens a door on the whole creative process. He gets things in perspective. We are not just dealing with certain events in Palestine 2,000 years ago: we are concerned with the purpose of God in history. The meaning of life and the universe is not '42', as the *Hitch Hiker's Guide to the Galaxy* facetiously claims. Understanding is disclosed through the 'Word'. That is how God displays his nature and how he is known. All this is proclaimed in the opening words of this amazing Gospel.

We perceive and know through our senses: hearing, sight, smell, touch and taste. For John, the basis of perception is the 'Word' – the mind or 'essence' of God. The 'Word' is the conveyor of life and meaning. Without the 'Word' nothing is understood, and if it is not understood then it might as well not exist (v. 3). The 'Word' illuminates and enlivens creation. Constantly available, it is there for those who will receive it – rather like radio waves or television signals. They are all around us, but we need to switch on our receivers before we can tune in to their message. For those with difficulty in tuning their sets, God has sent an engineer – a TV evangelist by the name of John the Baptist. He will show us how to switch on and select our programme. The function of an evangelist is to convey good news, to ensure it is understood and to witness to its veracity. This is precisely the role of the writer of this Gospel. Ingeniously, he projects these same characteristics on the Baptist (vv. 6–8).

Once we have received the transmission, we may suffer interference. Sadly, there is in the airways a jamming system set to block or distort the signal we are receiving. The evangelist identifies this interference in verse 5 as *darkness* and again in verse 10 as *the world*. We shall encounter both these concepts throughout the Gospel. Both interfere with the signal by trying to either distort it or reject it. At the onset we are warned that the message or revelation does not have an easy passage, but there is the promise of great reward for those who persevere.

Those with good reception and understanding will be given power to become 'children of God' (v. 12). Suddenly, it will become clear and the penny will drop. The picture will come into focus. We shall not only hear the 'Word', we shall see, taste, touch and smell it. For the 'Word' will become flesh and even 'pitch a tent' with us (v. 14). Then we shall know grace and truth in all its fullness. We shall even 'see' or 'understand' the very nature of God as he has been made known in Jesus Christ (v. 17), the one who is in the bosom of the Father (v. 18). This is the great theme of John's Gospel – perceiving, 'seeing' and understanding. He will provide us with a series of clues, signposts and pointers, so that we may believe and know Jesus Christ as the revealer of God and in believing this, we may have life in his name (20.31).

- In Genesis I the first word that God utters is to call light into being. Is it possible for us to distinguish and separate the light from the dark in our lives?

- Is there anyone around like John the Baptist to help us see the difference?

- How do we become more receptive people? Will it involve us seeing things differently?

- This passage (John 1.1–18) is often read at Christmas services. How does it relate to Luke's story of there being no room at the inn?

- Notice the similarities between how Mark opens his Gospel and how John begins his: 'The beginning of the gospel of Jesus Christ the Son of God' (1.1). They both announce who Jesus is. How important is it for us to be clear as to the identity of Jesus?

2

John the Baptist makes an opening

John 1.19–34

[19]Now this was John's testimony when the Jews of Jerusalem sent priests and Levites to ask him who he was. [20]He did not fail to confess, but confessed freely, 'I am not the Christ.'

[21]They asked him, 'Then who are you? Are you Elijah?'

He said, 'I am not.'

'Are you the Prophet?'

He answered, 'No.'

[22]Finally they said, 'Who are you? Give us an answer to take back to those who sent us. What do you say about yourself?'

[23]John replied in the words of Isaiah the prophet, 'I am the voice of one calling in the desert, "Make straight the way for the Lord."'

[24]Now some Pharisees who had been sent [25]questioned him, 'Why then do you baptise if you are not the Christ, nor Elijah, nor the Prophet?'

[26]'I baptise with water,' John replied, 'but among you stands one you do not know. [27]He is the one who comes after me, the thongs of whose sandals I am not worthy to untie.'

[28]This all happened at Bethany on the other side of the Jordan, where John was baptising. [29]The next day John saw Jesus coming towards him and said, 'Look, the Lamb of God, who takes away the sin of the world! [30]This is the one I meant when I said, "A man who comes after me has surpassed me because he was before me." [31]I myself did not know him, but the reason I came baptising with water was that he might be revealed to Israel.'

[32]Then John gave this testimony: 'I saw the Spirit come down from heaven as a dove and remain on him. [33]I would not have known him, except that the one who sent me to baptise with water told me, "The man on whom you see the Spirit come down and remain is he who will baptise with the Holy Spirit." [34]I have seen and I testify that this is the Son of God.'

John the Baptist is an enigma. What purpose does he fulfil in the proclamation of this gospel and what is his relation to Jesus? The evangelist has him answer these questions for himself, mostly in the negative: 'I am not the Christ (v. 20), not Elijah nor the Prophet, merely a voice crying in the wilderness' (v. 23). This voice can be found in the other Gospels (e.g. Mark 1.2–3). John the Baptist's role is to prepare the way for a new beginning. The prophet Isaiah, whom he quotes, was speaking of the exiles returning home to the promised land. John the Baptist is speaking in terms of a new exodus, one in which the people will be led out of slavery and blindness to the truth. The fourth evangelist presents John the Baptist in a very focused role. Here we have no description of his baptismal ministry.

The Baptist is perceptive enough. Unlike his portrait in the synoptic Gospels, John the Baptist has no qualms about declaring who Jesus is. He is also very keen to impress this on his followers. He is not even described as 'the Baptist', nor is there a mention of him baptizing Jesus. All he does is tune the set into the 'Jesus programme'. Because he is so open to the Spirit he will open the minds of others to Jesus. At the time of writing, there may well have been a dispute between the community that produced this Gospel and those who still revered the Baptist. This presentation is meant to clarify the role of the Baptist as a faithful witness to Jesus. Unlike the picture of Peter at the trial before Caiaphas (18.15–24), the Baptist remains resolute in his testimony to Jesus. In a matter of six verses we are told that for the Baptist, Jesus precedes him, is Spirit empowered and is both the Son and Lamb of God. We are dealing here with something more than the Messiah, and the Baptist is the first to openly proclaim it.

There does seem to be a policy of 'downplaying' the importance of John the Baptist in the Fourth Gospel. Every Gospel begins with a mention of John the Baptist. He was known to the Jewish historian Josephus. He is also mentioned in the speeches in Acts which summarize the main events in the life of Jesus. The fact that Jesus was baptized by John might suggest that the Baptist was in some way superior. If there was such an opinion circulating, the Fourth Gospel was very keen to put the matter straight. Verses 27 and 30 both emphasize the Baptist's inferior role. The Church continues this tradition by marking his feast on 24 June. From this date the days will get shorter. The Baptist must decrease and Jesus must increase (4.30).

- **Why do you think that the fourth evangelist is keen to focus on John the Baptist as a witness?**

- Does Jesus point beyond himself to God?

- What does John mean by describing Jesus as 'the Lamb of God who takes away the sins of the world'?

- Many paintings of John the Baptist show him pointing to Jesus. How might we point beyond ourselves to Jesus?

- Does the Baptist begin to open doors on our understanding of who Jesus is?

3

The Door Opens
for the First Disciples

John 1.35–51

³⁵**The next day John was there again with two of his disciples.** ³⁶When he saw Jesus passing by, he said, 'Look, the Lamb of God!' ³⁷When the two disciples heard him say this, they followed Jesus. ³⁸Turning round, Jesus saw them following and asked, 'What do you want?'

They said, 'Rabbi' (which means Teacher), 'where are you staying?'

³⁹'Come,' he replied, 'and you will see.' So they went and saw where he was staying, and spent that day with him. It was about the tenth hour.

⁴⁰Andrew, Simon Peter's brother, was one of the two who heard what John had said and who had followed Jesus. ⁴¹The first thing Andrew did was to find his brother Simon and tell him, 'We have found the Messiah' (that is, the Christ). ⁴²And he brought him to Jesus.

Jesus looked at him and said, 'You are Simon son of John. You will be called Cephas' (which, when translated, is Peter).

⁴³The next day Jesus decided to leave for Galilee. Finding Philip, he said to him, 'Follow me.'

⁴⁴Philip, like Andrew and Peter, was from the town of Bethsaida. ⁴⁵Philip found Nathanael and told him, 'We have found the one Moses wrote about in the Law, and about whom the prophets also wrote—Jesus of Nazareth, the son of Joseph.'

⁴⁶'Nazareth! Can anything good come from there?' Nathanael asked.

'Come and see,' said Philip.

⁴⁷When Jesus saw Nathanael approaching, he said of him, 'Here is a true Israelite, in whom there is nothing false.'

⁴⁸'How do you know me?' Nathanael asked.

Jesus answered, 'I saw you while you were still under the fig-tree before Philip called you.'

⁴⁹Then Nathanael declared, 'Rabbi, you are the Son of God; you are the King of Israel.'

⁵⁰Jesus said, 'You believe because I told you I saw you under the fig-tree. You shall see greater things than that.' ⁵¹He then added, 'I tell you the truth, you shall see heaven open, and the angels of God ascending and descending on the Son of Man.'

The progression of days continues to the end of this chapter. This is now the third day of our story. It was on the third day that the resurrection clarified and affirmed that Jesus was raised by the Father

7

as his beloved Son. On this third day the evangelist has the Baptist testifying that Jesus is the beloved Son in whom the Father delights, 'Behold the Lamb of God'. This time it is not a general statement but aimed at his own disciples. The Baptist continues to point to Jesus at the expense of his own following. Immediately a door is opened and two of his own disciples follow Jesus. There then occurs the first of many dialogues between Jesus and those that follow him. He asks them what they are looking for. This same question Jesus asked of Mary Magdalene in the garden on the third day after the crucifixion. 'Rabbi', meaning teacher, uses the same form of address for Jesus as Mary does in John 20.16. In the Fourth Gospel Jesus is the Teacher who leads everyone who seeks for truth.

The way John tells the story of the first disciples reminds us of the calling of the disciples in Mark's Gospel. Two seekers are invited to 'come and see' (v. 39): crucial words for the fourth evangelist. Those who want to know God must make a pilgrimage of faith and have their eyes opened to the truth.

Although John and Mark do not tell the same story they often make the same theological point. Here they both emphasize that discipleship is defined in terms of fellowship with Jesus. For Mark, a disciple is one who is 'with Jesus' (Mark 3.14). Here we have the first two disciples spending time with Jesus, staying with him for a whole day. This day is going to be the first of many in which the disciples will be illuminated by their new teacher, one who will open the doors of their perceptions. Again we are reminded of the first Easter Day when the disciples embarked on a new form of existence, one they had to share with others. Simon Peter is sent for in both accounts. Here he is given a new name, Cephas (v. 42), and a new identity.

The following day Jesus is in Galilee and calls Philip, who continues to draw others into the circle. Nathanael is less than compliant. He represents those whose minds are closed to the possibility of new insights. His prejudice against there being anything good emerging from such an insignificant place as Nazareth is only overcome by the openness of Philip's direct invitation to 'come and see' (v. 46). Taking up the offer, Nathanael is astonished at how well Jesus knows him. 'Knowing and seeing' are equated in the text. Nathanael may be blinded by prejudice, but this is contrasted with the perception of Jesus. He can see into Nathanael's soul. He describes Nathanael as an Israelite in whom there is no deceit. This prompts Nathanael to open his heart and mind to the truth, and he makes a full confession of faith equal to that of another sceptic, Thomas, at the end of the Gospel (20.29). However, greater things than this will be seen by those with the eyes of faith. They will see heaven opened and perceive their own destiny as disciples of the Son of Man (v. 51).

- Note the role played by Andrew in bringing his brother Simon and the others to Jesus. What can we learn from this style of evangelism?

- In what sense are we able to 'come and see' before we can really know what it is we are putting our faith in?

- How can we encourage others to 'come and see' what it is that Christians share?

- How important is the idea of 'family' in Christian evangelism?

4

Opening Sign: Water Turns to Wine

John 2.1–12

¹**On the third day a wedding took place at Cana in Galilee.** Jesus' mother was there, ²and Jesus and his disciples had also been invited to the wedding. ³When the wine was gone, Jesus' mother said to him, 'They have no more wine.'

⁴'Dear woman, why do you involve me?' Jesus replied, 'My time has not yet come.'

⁵His mother said to the servants, 'Do whatever he tells you.'

⁶Nearby stood six stone water jars, the kind used by the Jews for ceremonial washing, each holding from twenty to thirty gallons.

⁷Jesus said to the servants, 'Fill the jars with water'; so they filled them to the brim.

⁸Then he told them, 'Now draw some out and take it to the master of the banquet.'

They did so, ⁹and the master of the banquet tasted the water that had been turned into wine. He did not realise where it had come from, though the servants who had drawn the water knew. Then he called the bridegroom aside ¹⁰and said, 'Everyone brings out the choice wine first and then the cheaper wine after the guests have had too much to drink; but you have saved the best till now.'

¹¹This, the first of his miraculous signs, Jesus performed at Cana in Galilee. He thus revealed his glory, and his disciples put their faith in him.

¹²After this he went down to Capernaum with his mother and brothers and his disciples. There they stayed for a few days.

We have noticed that John is keen to provide a number of clues or pointers as to the identity of Jesus. Here we have the first official 'sign' (v. 11). It occurs in the company of Jesus' disciples and in the presence of his mother. The only other reference to a gathering of this kind is found in Acts 2 when Mary and the disciples are together in the upper room about to be filled with the Holy Spirit at Pentecost. There are a number of links – both stories are about new beginnings and both use the image of wine to suggest the joyful spirit of the Gospel. The results are intoxicating. The generous provision is spectacular and overwhelming.

A wedding is itself a celebration of a new beginning. John tells us that this one also took place on 'the third day', another reference to the resurrection story. The disciples have been promised an open heaven (v. 51). Now they are witnessing the marriage of heaven and earth in the actions of Jesus as he reluctantly provides them with a sign of who he is. Again we seem to hear Markan echoes in the text of John. In Mark, Jesus is so reluctant to disclose his identity that the term 'Messianic Secret' has been coined to describe his reticence. Jesus is less reticent in John, but his reluctance here is explained in terms of 'his hour not yet having come'. This phrase is also used in Mark, when it refers to the passion of Jesus in which the true nature of God's love will be displayed. For John this is described in terms of 'glorification'. Jesus in this passage is not ready for that sort of identification, so he resists his mother's attempt to push him forward too soon. There is a tension between disclosure and hiddenness which is developed throughout this Gospel. Jesus will often play a game of 'hide and seek' with those who are looking for him.

There is a hint of irritation between mother and son here which may also be noticed in Luke's story of the finding in the temple (Luke 2.48) and in the odd story in Mark when his mother and brothers try to restrain him (Mark 3.31). It is certain that Mary, who is not named in John, precipitates this disclosure as Jesus reluctantly turns water into wine in vast quantities, equivalent to two to three thousand modern wine glasses!

Mark has a reference to wine in the context of new and old wineskins (Mark 2.22). The same theme is dealt with here. This story is a sign that what Jesus represents is far richer and more significant than anything that was tasted under the old dispensation – indicated by the six stone jars of purification (v. 6). The best wine has been kept until now (v. 10). For now, the Word has been made flesh and dwells among us. The enriching, challenging, joyful presence of God in Jesus is present at a country wedding. This is cause for great celebration and will result in a disclosure. The disciples who see what this sign signifies believe in him, and this will eventually burst the old wineskins. This sign points to the coming break between the infant Church and Judaism. Intoxicated by the Spirit, the new community of faith will break with the old ways of Judaism.

- Why does Jesus refer to his mother as 'woman'? Is he being disrespectful to his mother and showing his irritation, or might there be another explanation?

- The mother of Jesus is not 'put down' by his reply to her request. Do you think her actions were justified in the light of subsequent events?

- How do you see the split between Christianity and Judaism: as quarrel or as the parting of two irreconcilable forces?

- What do you think is meant by the phrase 'my hour has not yet come'?

5

Jesus Fires an Opening Shot

John 2.13–25

13When it was almost time for the Jewish Passover, Jesus went up to Jerusalem. 14In the temple courts he found men selling cattle, sheep and doves, and others sitting at tables exchanging money. 15So he made a whip out of cords, and drove all from the temple area, both sheep and cattle; he scattered the coins of the money changers and overturned their tables. 16To those who sold doves he said, 'Get these out of here! How dare you turn my Father's house into a market!'

17His disciples remembered that it is written, 'Zeal for your house will consume me.'

18Then the Jews demanded of him, 'What miraculous sign can you show us to prove your authority to do all this?'

19Jesus answered them, 'Destroy this temple, and I will raise it again in three days.'

20The Jews replied, 'It has taken forty-six years to build this temple, and you are going to raise it in three days?' 21But the temple he had spoken of was his body. 22After he was raised from the dead, his disciples recalled what he had said. Then they believed the Scripture and the words that Jesus had spoken.

23Now while he was in Jerusalem at the Passover Feast, many people saw the miraculous signs he was doing and believed in his name. 24But Jesus would not entrust himself to them, for he knew all men. 25He did not need man's testimony about man, for he knew what was in a man.

Whereas the other Gospels have the cleansing of the temple story at the end of Jesus' ministry, John has the incident happening at the beginning. Why? The answer may be related to John's keenness to develop his theme of Jesus being new direct access to God. He has shown us a Jesus who has commanded the respect and devotion of John the Baptist, who pointed to him as the one who takes away sin. We have seen that Jesus has disclosed something of his 'glory' in that he has transformed the water of the old covenant into the wine of the new covenant. He can now be seen to replace the need for a temple.

This Jewish temple, as re-built under Herod the Great, was one of the wonders of the ancient world. Recent archaeological excavations are showing the extent of these huge buildings before their destruction in AD 70. For the Jewish nation, the temple was the focus of their devotion and the place where God had caused 'his name to dwell'. The concept of a God who pitched his tent with his people in the wilderness was formalized by the building of this more permanent house of God by King Solomon. Although the temple had been destroyed and rebuilt several times, it still had a powerful hold on the Jewish imagination. It is a great credit to Judaism that the Jewish faith survived the destruction of this shrine.

Jesus, in taking a 'whip hand' to all that clutters and clatters in the temple precinct, is not just demonstrating his abhorrence of commercialism. He is condemning a system that complicates access to God. The 'Jews' now appear on the scene for the first time, demanding a sign. (We are reminded of the question asked of Jesus by the chief priests: 'By what authority do you do these things?' – Matthew 21.23.) The only sign that Jesus gives is the passion, the destruction of his body and its raising up in three days. Jesus is the new temple, the focus of God where God has caused his name to dwell. He is the new Bethel ('House of God'), he is the 'Son of Man', the open door to heaven where angels ascend and descend (1.51). As yet the disciples do not fully understand these things. Those who do respond do so for the wrong motives (v. 25). After the resurrection when Jesus is fully glorified, they will make the connections that John has made in this narrative.

- **How dependent is our idea of God on structures and institutions of the Church?**

- **Are maintenance of the Church and mission necessarily opposites?**

- **What impediments do we put in the way of direct access to God through Jesus Christ?**

- **What do you think constitutes the Church: the building or the gathered community or both?**

- **In this passage John talks of the body of Jesus replacing the temple. Do you think the destruction of the temple was necessary to enable the Church to emerge as the body of Christ?**

THE DEBATE BEGINS

6

Nicodemus Opens a Discussion

John 3.1–21

¹**Now there was a man of the Pharisees** named Nicodemus, a member of the Jewish ruling council. ²He came to Jesus at night and said, 'Rabbi, we know you are a teacher who has come from˙ God. For no-one could perform the miraculous signs you are doing if God were not with him.' ³In reply Jesus declared, 'I tell you the truth, no-one can see the kingdom of God unless he is born again.'

⁴'How can a man be born when he is old?' Nicodemus asked. 'Surely he cannot enter a second time into his mother's womb to be born!'

⁵Jesus answered, 'I tell you the truth, no-one can enter the kingdom of God unless he is born of water and the Spirit. ⁶Flesh gives birth to flesh, but the Spirit gives birth to spirit. ⁷You should not be surprised at my saying, "You must be born again." ⁸The wind blows wherever it pleases. You hear its sound, but you cannot tell where it comes from or where it is going. So it is with everyone born of the Spirit.'

⁹'How can this be?' Nicodemus asked.

¹⁰'You are Israel's teacher,' said Jesus, 'and do you not understand these things? ¹¹I tell you the truth, we speak of what we know, and we testify to what we have seen, but still you people do not accept our testimony. ¹²I have spoken to you of earthly things and you do not believe; how then will you believe if I speak of heavenly things? ¹³No-one has ever gone into heaven except the one who came from heaven—the Son of Man. ¹⁴Just as Moses lifted up the snake in the desert, so the Son of Man must be lifted up, ¹⁵that everyone who believes in him may have eternal life.

¹⁶'For God so loved the world that he gave his one and only Son, that whoever believes in him shall not perish but have eternal life. ¹⁷For God did not send his Son into the world to condemn the world, but to save the world through him. ¹⁸Whoever believes in him is not condemned, but whoever does not believe stands condemned already because he has not

believed in the name of God's one and only Son. [19]This is the verdict: Light has come into the world, but men loved darkness instead of light because their deeds were evil. [20]Everyone who does evil hates the light, and will not come into the light for fear that his deeds will be exposed. [21]But whoever lives by the truth comes into the light, so that it may be seen plainly that what he has done has been done through God.'

Darkness, as we have seen (1.5), is an important feature in this Gospel, which promises light. In this scene a 'ruler of the Jews' named Nicodemus comes to Jesus by night, under cover of darkness, with an enquiry. Nicodemus seems to represent those in the community who are attracted to Jesus, but as yet are not fully tuned in to who he was, and what he represents. They have not recognized him as the 'light of the world'. We need to remember that this Gospel comes from a situation in which there is a breakdown in relationships between Jews and Christians. Many in the Christian party have been expelled from the synagogue because of their belief in Jesus as the Messiah. We shall come across a number of allusions to this in the text. Such a painful situation is rather like a family row. There will be those who choose to sit on the fence, those who try to do secret deals and those who indulge in special pleading. As far as John is concerned, things have gone far enough. It is time for a decision.

This passage illustrates, in dramatic terms, the necessity for decision and commitment. Nicodemus's flattery is probably ironic. He tries to ingratiate himself with Jesus with what may be empty words but are in fact a summary of the truth. This device often occurs in John. Jesus ignores this deviousness and gets straight to the point. The phrase 'Truly, truly' emphasizes the solemnity of what he has to say. 'Unless you are born from above, you cannot enter the Kingdom of God' (v. 3). The prologue tells us (1.13) that those who receive the Word are 'born of God'. In other words, an entirely new outlook is required for those who wish to see God's Kingdom here on earth. Heaven is open for those who can see (1.51). The Word is made flesh for those who can perceive grace and truth (1.14).

Sadly, Nicodemus doesn't get the message. He, like many in a position of authority, can only hear and see the mundane. They have only a 'this-worldly' view of reality. So Jesus talks further about what is required for those who wish to see and enter the Kingdom of God (vv. 5–8). In the plainest terms he distinguishes between the material and the spiritual. The 'flesh' represents a limited and restricted outlook. The 'Spirit' is about freedom and openness. Access is gained by water and spirit – a clear reference to the life-changing effects of baptism which Paul develops in Romans 5. Nicodemus's reply, 'How can this be?', is reminiscent of Nathanael's reply (1.46). Again Jesus talks in terms of a bridge between heaven an earth and about his own role in achieving this; hinting darkly at his own death in the process (vv. 14–15).

A bright beam of light is shining which will expose the truth of God as it is seen in Jesus. What is that truth? This is the question Pilate will ask, but he will have no interest in knowing the answer. The truth is the witness of Jesus to a God who offers life to those who will receive it (vv. 16–17).

- **Nicodemus has a limited perception of who Jesus is and what he stands for. Does this imply that powerful people often have special difficulty in understanding Jesus' purpose and mission?**

- **Do we share his limitations? Can we answer these questions about Jesus' purpose and mission?**

- **Nicodemus is an authority figure – 'a ruler' and 'a teacher'. Is he typical of those in authority today?**

- **How do we sharpen our perceptions of the distinction between flesh and spirit?**

- **What connection do you see between the lifting up of Jesus and eternal life?**

- **In what way would you define eternal life?**

7

The Baptist Bows Out

John 3.22–36

²²After this, Jesus and his disciples went out into the Judean countryside, where he spent some time with them, and baptised. **²³Now John also was baptising at Aenon near Salim, because there was plenty of water, and people were constantly coming to be baptised. ²⁴(This was before John was put in prison.) ²⁵An argument developed between some of John's disciples and a certain Jew over the matter of ceremonial washing. ²⁶They came to John and said to him, 'Rabbi, that man who was with you on the other side of the Jordan—the one you testified about—well, he is baptising, and everyone is going to him.' ²⁷To this John replied, 'A man can receive only what is given him from heaven. ²⁸You yourselves can testify that I said, "I am not the Christ but am sent ahead of him." ²⁹The bride belongs to the bridegroom. The friend who attends the bridegroom waits and listens for him, and is full of joy when he hears the bridegroom's voice. That joy is mine, and it is now complete. ³⁰He must become greater; I must become less.

³¹'The one who comes from above is above all; the one who is from the earth belongs to the earth, and speaks as one from the earth. The one who comes from heaven is above all. ³²He testifies to what he has seen and heard, but no-one accepts his testimony. ³³The man who has accepted it has certified that God is truthful. ³⁴For the one whom God has sent speaks the words of God, for God gives the Spirit without limit. ³⁵The Father loves the Son and has placed everything in his hands. ³⁶Whoever believes in the Son has eternal life, but whoever rejects the Son will not see life, for God's wrath remains on him.'

This is a puzzling passage. We have an odd reference to Jesus and his disciples baptizing in Judea (v. 22). We have the Baptist testifying and baptizing (v. 23). A Jew appears asking a question about purifying (the same word that is used of the stone jars at the Wedding in Cana – 2.6). Then these characters disappear, and the Baptist launches on his last speech. But where does it end? – at verse 30? – or does it continue to the end of this chapter? My own feeling is for a 'decreased' version of the speech ending at verse 30. The last five verses thus become the fourth evangelist giving his editorial summary of this chapter.

The writer of this Gospel is constantly concerned to explain who he believes Jesus to be. The technical term for this is 'Christology'. John is reckoned to have a very 'elevated' Christology, presenting Jesus as a divine Saviour. It is claimed that he is less interested in the human attributes of Jesus than the writers of other Gospels. I am not convinced that this is a fair description of his intentions. It is only John who tells us that Jesus weeps over his friend (11.35). Certainly, he believes Jesus to be the Messiah from God – the Word made flesh, the true revealer of God. But he is also concerned to present a true picture of God himself. For him, Jesus is the key to our understanding of God. We no longer need the law or the temple to open a door so that we might gain access to God. Somehow Jesus has made him known, for he utters the words of God (v. 34). He is of heaven, and bears witness to what he has seen (v. 32). No one may have seen God, but the enfleshed Word has made him known (1.18). These issues will be developed in the rest of the Gospel. Here the evangelist is testifying to his belief that to have seen and heard Jesus is to have experienced God himself.

The veracity of this testimony is recognized by the Baptist, who is perceptive enough to know that Jesus' authority is heaven sent (v. 27). All those who accept this testimony are united with Jesus through baptism. Like Mark, and much of the New Testament, John's Gospel is concerned to demonstrate what becoming a Christian involves. Those who receive Christ, attesting to him in their baptismal promises, are united to him, enjoying the first fruits of his relationship with the Father. They see God, as Jesus sees him. 'For he has made him known' (1.18). In seeing God, they experience eternal life. Those who do not believe are disobedient to the will of God and experience 'wrath' or the obverse side of this life. The puzzle for this writer and for many of us today is, it still seems as if 'no one receives his testimony' (v. 32).

- Is it possible that John's church fellowship were experiencing difficulties in agreeing who Jesus was, and what he came to achieve? Does this throw some light on the passage?

- Is it important for us to get our Christology sorted out? What do you think Jesus' relation to the Father was, and is? How does it affect us? What effect does doctrine have on our behaviour?

- What does being a Christian mean for us today?

- Do you think there were some early Christians who might have preferred a less exalted picture of Jesus as a 'prophet from God'?

8

The Samaritan Woman
Opens a Debate

John 4.1–26

¹**The Pharisees heard that Jesus was** gaining and baptising more disciples than John, ²although in fact it was not Jesus who baptised, but his disciples. ³When the Lord learned of this, he left Judea and went back once more to Galilee.

⁴Now he had to go through Samaria. ⁵So he came to a town in Samaria called Sychar, near the plot of ground Jacob had given to his son Joseph. ⁶Jacob's well was there, and Jesus, tired as he was from the journey, sat down by the well. It was about the sixth hour.

⁷When a Samaritan woman came to draw water, Jesus said to her, 'Will you give me a drink?' ⁸(His disciples had gone into the town to buy food.)

⁹The Samaritan woman said to him, 'You are a Jew and I am a Samaritan woman. How can you ask me for a drink?' (For Jews do not associate with Samaritans.)

¹⁰Jesus answered her, 'If you knew the gift of God and who it is that asks you for a drink, you would have asked him and he would have given you living water.'

¹¹'Sir,' the woman said, 'you have nothing to draw with and the well is deep. Where can you get this living water? ¹²Are you greater than our father Jacob, who gave us the well and drank from it himself, as did also his sons and his flocks and herds?'

¹³Jesus answered, 'Everyone who drinks this water will be thirsty again, ¹⁴but whoever drinks the water I give him will never thirst. Indeed, the water I give him will become in him a spring of water welling up to eternal life.'

¹⁵The woman said to him, 'Sir, give me this water so that I won't get thirsty and have to keep coming here to draw water.'

¹⁶He told her, 'Go, call your husband and come back.'

¹⁷'I have no husband,' she replied.

Jesus said to her, 'You are right when you say you have no husband. ¹⁸The fact is, you have had five husbands, and the man you now have is not your husband. What you have just said is quite true.'

¹⁹'Sir,' the woman said, 'I can see that you are a prophet. ²⁰Our fathers worshipped on this mountain, but you Jews claim that the place where we must worship is in Jerusalem.'

²¹Jesus declared, 'Believe me, woman, a time is coming when you will worship the Father neither on this mountain nor in Jerusalem. ²²You Samaritans worship what you do not know; we worship what we do know, for salvation is from the Jews. ²³Yet a time is coming and has now come when the true worshippers will worship the Father in spirit and truth, for they are the kind of wor-

shippers the Father seeks. [24]God is spirit, and his worshippers must worship in spirit and in truth.'
[25]The woman said, 'I know that Messiah' (called Christ) 'is coming. When he comes, he will explain everything to us.'
[26]Then Jesus declared, 'I who speak to you am he.'

This passage contains one of the longest dialogues in the New Testament. Surprisingly, the conversation is not between Jesus and a male disciple, but with a woman, and a Samaritan woman at that. Before we discuss their conversation and what it means, there is a rather strange reference to baptism to deal with. We are told in verse 1 that Jesus was baptizing and making more disciples than the Baptist. This indeed is given as the reason for Jesus' removal from Judea (v. 3). There is no other reference to Jesus baptizing in the New Testament. The evangelist seems to contradict himself by stating that Jesus did not actually do the baptizing, only his disciples (v. 2). How do we explain this? Could it be that we have an addition to the text, or is it that there is such a connection between discipleship and baptism that the distinction is blurred. The puzzle remains. However, whatever the answer, it is the cause of Jesus passing through Samaria on his journey to Galilee.

We know from the historian Josephus that many Jews travelled through Samaria, despite its obvious risks, akin to sectarian groups marching through the residential districts of their opponents today. John suggests that it was part of God's plan that Jesus took this route, so the meeting at the well has great significance. It is difficult for us to imagine a more improbable meeting and subsequent conversation. Even today in the Middle East, men and women rarely converse in public. Sworn enemies are even more unlikely to fall into conversation in this way. A Jewish rabbi would certainly not ask a Samaritan woman for a drink – and remember this is no ordinary Samaritan woman! By coming to the well at midday she shows herself to be alienated from her fellow women, who would normally draw water early and late in the day when the sun is not at its height. Her lifestyle with a history of multiple liaisons, which is the cause of her alienation, is referred to by Jesus in verse 18. The story from now on is loaded in symbolism. This is Jacob's well. Jacob had a personality change when he encountered God wrestling with him in the form of an angel. As a result of this, both his name and his personality were changed. Jacob became 'Israel', which means 'one who wrestled with God'. This alienated woman unknowingly strives with God in Jesus in such a way as to change her life. It will all happen near the place where Jacob saw an open heaven, bridged with angels ascending and descending on a ladder. Jesus makes a bridge, not just between Jews and Samaritans, but between heaven and earth. All this is achieved by the provision of 'living water'.

At first the woman, like Nicodemus, does not understand. She begins the discussion by being closed-minded. She is fixed on material provision, making reference to things as they are (the well is deep – v. 11) and to the way they have always been (her devotion to Jacob the Samaritan patriarch – v. 12). Jesus is able to raise her mind from the merely material and open her to the eternal. He is contrasting what he has to offer with the Samaritan tradition and its places of worship. In overcoming the externals of religious differences Jesus has broken down the division between Jew and non-Jew. What he has to offer transcends ritual. Those who follow this teaching will 'worship God in spirit and in truth' (v. 24). They will find that in coming to Jesus they will receive life-giving water. The enmity between Jews and Samaritans seemed unbridgeable, 'for Jews had no dealings with Samaritans' (v. 9). Yet we know that some of the first Christians were able to overcome this enmity, and accept each other in Christ.

- In what way can insights from this passage and Luke's story of the Good Samaritan help heal the divisions in our society today?

- Is there a message in this simple request of Jesus for a drink? Are we sometimes too proud to make the first move for fear of being snubbed or even rejected?

- Jesus exposes the reason for the woman's isolation, and in so doing refers to the historical causes for the breakdown in relations between Jews and Samaritans. (The Jews accused the Samaritans of making irregular liaisons.) Is it important and necessary for us to face the truth about our divisions?

- Jesus is at pains to draw the woman and the community to him as the source of life and meaning. Should our concern to worship God in spirit and in truth override all other considerations? That is to say, are we willing to change and focus on the offer Christ makes?

9

A Samaritan Harvest

John 4.27–42

²⁷**Just then his disciples returned and were** surprised to find him talking with a woman. But no-one asked, 'What do you want?' or 'Why are you talking with her?' ²⁸Then, leaving her water jar, the woman went back to the town and said to the people, ²⁹'Come, see a man who told me everything I ever did. Could this be the Christ?' ³⁰They came out of the town and made their way towards him.

³¹Meanwhile his disciples urged him, 'Rabbi, eat something.'

³²But he said to them, 'I have food to eat that you know nothing about.'

³³Then his disciples said to each other, 'Could someone have brought him food?'

³⁴'My food,' said Jesus, 'is to do the will of him who sent me and to finish his work. ³⁵Do you not say, "Four months more and then the harvest"? I tell you, open your eyes and look at the fields! They are ripe for harvest.

³⁶Even now the reaper draws his wages, even now he harvests the crop for eternal life, so that the sower and the reaper may be glad together. ³⁷Thus the saying "One sows and another reaps" is true. ³⁸I sent you to reap what you have not worked for. Others have done the hard work, and you have reaped the benefits of their labour.'

³⁹Many of the Samaritans from that town believed in him because of the woman's testimony, 'He told me everything I ever did.' ⁴⁰So when the Samaritans came to him, they urged him to stay with them, and he stayed two days. ⁴¹And because of his words many more became believers.

⁴²They said to the woman, 'We no longer believe just because of what you said; now we have heard for ourselves, and we know that this man really is the Saviour of the world.'

The disciples return only to find their master talking to the equivalent to 'the town tart'. Their sense of embarrassment is almost palpable in the text (v. 27). They restrain themselves from asking about the incident as the woman makes off for the town leaving behind that symbolic water jar that we have met before at the wedding feast. She has abandoned the old dependencies and certainties that this symbolizes. She is now free from her fear of meeting the neighbours and indeed publishes abroad the open invitation to 'come and see' (v. 29). The same words that were encountered in chapter 1 (v. 39 and v. 46), adding that this 'may be the Christ'. How has this woman come to this conviction? She began in a surly enough way, treating Jesus as a precocious stranger. Then she affords him the respect due to a Rabbi, 'Sir' (v. 15), and ends proclaiming he might be the Christ! So forceful is her invitation that the townsfolk respond to her testimony and come to see for themselves. Their invitation to Jesus to stay with them (v. 40) is all the more remarkable, as is their astonishing confession that Jesus is 'the Saviour of the World' (v. 42). (Note how the invitation, 'stay with us,' resulting in a conviction about Jesus, is parallel to the experience of the Emmaus disciples in Luke 24.)

The disciples are as puzzled as we may be with all this. They ask Jesus to eat, but Jesus talks about other sustenance (doing God's will and, more significantly, accomplishing his work (v. 34). Is John fast-forwarding the mission of Jesus and incorporating an element of hindsight more to do with a later situation? Certainly, the fields are 'white for harvest' (v. 35). The time is ready and the work accomplished, for the Samaritans are already being gathered in by the woman's invitation to 'come and see' (v. 29). They are pre-figuring a golden age when all will be completed by Jesus' self-offering on the cross. Then, as now, Jesus is presented as the 'life-giver' pouring out his spirit in the guise of water and blood.

The woman came for ordinary water and was offered living water, welling up into eternal life. Jesus is the source, the spring of this life, giving spiritual sustenance. It is on this that he himself feeds (v. 34). The disciples are incorporated into this provision by reaping the benefits of what others have sown. They and the prophets stand in the same tradition of offering God's life to the world. All that is needed is for them to be receptive and open, to lift up their eyes and see the opportunity is at hand (v. 35). This is the response to be found in the Samaritan woman. Because of her openness to the gospel she recognized and responded to Jesus moving from earthly to heavenly insight. She, like a true disciple, shares this insight with others and openly invites them to make their own response. This they do, openly confessing Jesus to be the Saviour of the World and wanting to remain with him.

- The Samaritans represent those who feel themselves alienated from established religion. How do we seek to communicate with them?

- Jesus stopped by a well. Can we provide some kind of meeting point in our community where people might fall into conversation and discover something of the 'water welling up into eternal life'?

- Are 'the fields' still 'white, ripe for harvest'? Do we see an opportunity when it arises? If so, how do we enable today's disciples to 'lift up their eyes' and recognize this fact?

10

To Galilee, where a Centurion Sees a Sign

John 4.43–54

43After the two days he left for Galilee. 44(Now Jesus himself had pointed out that a prophet has no honour in his own country.) 45When he arrived in Galilee, the Galileans welcomed him. They had seen all that he had done in Jerusalem at the Passover Feast, for they also had been there. 46Once more he visited Cana in Galilee, where he had turned the water into wine. And there was a certain royal official whose son lay sick at Capernaum. 47When this man heard that Jesus had arrived in Galilee from Judea, he went to him and begged him to come and heal his son, who was close to death. 48'Unless you people see miraculous signs and wonders,' Jesus told him, 'you will never believe.'

49The royal official said, 'Sir, come down before my child dies.' 50Jesus replied, 'You may go. Your son will live.'

The man took Jesus at his word and departed. 51While he was still on the way, his servants met him with the news that his boy was living. 52When he enquired as to the time when his son got better, they said to him, 'The fever left him yesterday at the seventh hour.' 53Then the father realised that this was the exact time at which Jesus had said to him, 'Your son will live.' So he and all his household believed. 54This was the second miraculous sign that Jesus performed, having come from Judea to Galilee.

In this section there are tantalizing echoes from the synoptic Gospels. The saying 'a prophet has no honour in his own country' (v. 44) looks back to Mark 6.4. The story about the official's boy healed at a distance (vv. 46–53) can be compared to Luke 7.4–10.

The first echo is more difficult to understand. In Mark the saying about rejection helps explain Jesus' reception in Nazareth, his home town. In John's account, the saying seems to have little to do with Galilee where he is welcomed (v. 45) and more to do with Jerusalem, which he has left because of hostility from the Pharisees (4.1) and the Jews' reaction to the temple cleansing (2.13–21). Why does John present

Jerusalem as the home of Jesus, instead of Nazareth? Probably because Jerusalem is regarded as the home of the prophets. This is the place which is the focus of their message and its invariable rejection. Jesus will have no honour there as the prologue has warned us; 'he came to his own and his own received him not' (1.11). Rejected by Jerusalem, believed in Samaria, now he is welcomed in Galilee. This is the location for another opening, a place for a sign.

The second echo of the synoptics in this passage is the story of distance healing. Luke tells the story of a centurion's servant, John of an official's son. They are obviously variations on the same story. As one might expect, John makes significant use of his version of the story, calling it the second 'sign' or 'clue' as to who Jesus is and what is his mission. Astonishingly, both the first two signs take place in the same village, Cana. It was here that water was turned into wine. It is here that the gentile will recognize and believe that Jesus is the source of life. In both instances, the stories begin with a reluctant Jesus. Here, he tests the official's faith: 'unless you see signs and wonders you will not believe'(4.48). In this case, the word 'sign' is being used in an Old Testament sense, meaning overtly miraculous. Jesus has shown his suspicion of a faith based on the spectacular (2.23–5). A gentile proves his trust in Jesus by pressing his request. Jesus responds 'go, your son will live' (v. 50). By taking Jesus at his word, the official enjoys the benefit of that word, which brings life. At the end of chapter 6, Peter comes to the same conclusion: 'you have the words of eternal life'.

So far John has shown us a number of openings; windows are being punched into heaven. First a Jew (Nicodemus) enquires about being born again, then a Samaritan woman asks for the water of life, and now a gentile asks for life for his boy. His belief in the words of Jesus is the second sign that Jesus is offering God's life to a dead world.

- **Is Jesus without honour among his people today? Has the Church failed to recognize what he is saying to us about life and judgement?**

- **How much testing would our faith in Jesus stand? Do we require 'signs and wonders' or are we content with 'signs of life' in the community who recognize the significance of Jesus for today?**

• How institutionalized have we become towards prophets who might disturb our complacency? Who are the prophets of our day and age? Are they welcomed by some and rejected by others?

THINGS HAPPEN

The Third Sign:
An Opening at the Pool of Bethesda

John 5.1–9

¹Some time later, Jesus went up to Jerusalem for a feast of the Jews. ²Now there is in Jerusalem near the Sheep Gate a pool, which in Aramaic is called Bethesda and which is surrounded by five covered colonnades. ³Here a great number of disabled people used to lie—the blind, the lame, the paralysed—and they waited for the moving of the waters. ⁴From time to time an angel of the Lord would come down and stir up the waters. The first one into the pool after each such disturbance would be cured of whatever disease he had.] ⁵One who was there had been an invalid for thirty-eight years. ⁶When Jesus saw him lying there and learned that he had been in this condition for a long time, he asked him, 'Do you want to get well?' ⁷'Sir,' the invalid replied, 'I have no-one to help me into the pool when the water is stirred. While I am trying to get in, someone else goes down ahead of me.' ⁸Then Jesus said to him, 'Get up! Pick up your mat and walk' ⁹At once the man was cured; he picked up his mat and walked.

Here we have Jesus returning to Jerusalem for an unnamed feast. Though imprecise about the occasion, John goes into great detail about this miracle, which constitutes the third sign. He tells us about the pool and its location at the 'sheep gate'. That particular gate has long since vanished, but a sheep market is still conducted in that location near to the archaeological excavations of the pool, which largely fits John's description. The theme of water is again developed. Jesus has shown that he can transform it into wine as a demonstration of how he is replacing the old dispensation. He has been hailed by the Baptist as the one who baptizes with both water and the Spirit. He has made available life-giving water to the Samaritan villagers. Now, in this story, the water which is seen as a means of healing is superseded by the healing presence of Jesus.

John sets the scene artfully. A poor lame character has kept a pathetic vigil at this spot for thirty-eight years. He has come here daily in the vain hope of effecting a cure by getting into the healing waters at the moment their powers are made effective. Unfortunately, he has been constantly frustrated by a more agile or more determined contestant. So long has this sad charade gone on that a question arises concerning his seriousness about being healed. Jesus gets straight to the point and immediately asks the man, 'Do you want to be healed?' (v. 6). Has the man become so institutionalized, so complacent with his lot, that he has forgotten why he has come here on a daily basis? The man does not answer this question directly but instead complains of being friendless and alone. Is this the excuse he has constructed for himself to explain why he has not been cured?

The man is certainly portrayed as a slave to his situation. He has not attempted to move on or investigate other solutions to his long-term illness. He is in a state of inaction, preferring the 'status quo' to a change in tactic. He is now little more than a professional beggar. Why then is John telling this story and placing it here at the beginning of this section in which Jesus embarks on a journey through Judaism? It seems more than likely that the man is an emblem of the kind of fossilized Judaism that John's community are encountering. The inertia and inactivity of the man over such a long time seems to represent an unwillingness to enjoy the healing benefits of the water on offer. (Thirty-eight years might be the age of John's church and the length of time that the discussion between the two factions has gone on. Possibly we might have here a clue to the date of this Gospel – AD70, the year that Jerusalem was destroyed by the Romans.)

What is the water on offer? Is it the baptismal waters of Christian discipleship? If the baptismal rite itself is an inhibitor to the reluctant man, then Jesus offers his own miraculous healing to the man instead. Is this the meaning of this sign? Jesus displays the unconditional prodigality of God's saving love to such a feckless individual as this, who neither asks for, nor expresses thanks for, the healing he receives. The healing is offered in similar words to those found in Mark 2.11. In both stories the healing is not requested by the recipient and causes a strong reaction from the religious authorities, eventually resulting in a plot to destroy Jesus (John 6.18; Mark 3.6).

• **What is it that prevents us from developing and moving on in our faith and understanding? Do we lack the moral courage, confidence, conviction and trusting faith to take the risks involved in such a creative development? Are we too comfortable and too ready to take the soft option?**

• **Can we face the question that Jesus asks – do we really want to be healed?**

• **Do you think there are many people on the margins of society, in bed and breakfast accommodation and sleeping rough, who have not been encouraged to accept healing and forgiveness simply because society has forgotten them?**

12

The Cured Man Walks

John 5.10–18

The day on which this took place was a Sabbath, ¹⁰and so the Jews said to the man who had been healed, 'It is the Sabbath; the law forbids you to carry your mat.' ¹¹But he replied, 'The man who made me well said to me "Pick up your mat and walk."' ¹²So they asked him, 'Who is this fellow who told you to pick it up and walk?' ¹³The man who was healed had no idea who it was, for Jesus had slipped away into the crowd that was there. ¹⁴Later Jesus found him at the temple and said to him, 'See, you are well again. Stop sinning or something worse may happen to you.' ¹⁵The man went away and told the Jews that it was Jesus who had made him well.

¹⁶So, because Jesus was doing these things on the Sabbath, the Jews persecuted him. ¹⁷Jesus said to them, 'My Father is always at his work to this very day, and I, too, am working.' ¹⁸For this reason the Jews tried all the harder to kill him; not only was he breaking the Sabbath, but he was even calling God his own Father, making himself equal with God.

John does not diagnose the man's condition; he merely reports that a sick man was cured. For ease of identification we shall refer to the man as 'the paralytic'. The paralytic is shaken out of his complacency by the stern word of Jesus to take up his bed and walk. Aspects of this story can be compared with the parable of the sower in Mark. Like the seed that is 'rootless' (Mark 4.17), once the paralytic encounters trouble or persecution he quickly falls away. The 'Jews' quickly come upon the scene and confront the man with the charge of Sabbath-breaking. Like Adam in the garden of Eden, he passes the buck, blaming Jesus for his 'law-breaking'. He claims that he is simply following orders. This rather pathetic character, relieved by Jesus of nearly forty years of futility, is neither grateful nor changed by his healing. We may conclude by his presence in the temple that he was in some way still bound to his Jewish faith. John makes it very clear that the man has no knowledge of Jesus (v. 13). When the enigmatic Jesus reveals himself to the man later, reminding him of his new-found health and telling him to 'sin no more', he is unable to respond. Instead he informs on Jesus (v. 15). Poor thanks for the gift of new life. John states that this was the reason why the 'Jews' persecuted Jesus – for healing the ungrateful paralytic on the Sabbath day.

The drama of the story turns on the charge that Jesus was a Sabbath-breaker. This is an issue in all the Gospels and reflects the interests of the early Christian communities in their debates with Judaism. In the other Gospels Jesus pours contempt on such attitudes as this which condemn acts of healing on the Sabbath as a 'work'. Here the charge is taken more seriously and Jesus engages in a kind of rabbinical debate with his accusers. His defence is that his Father has never ceased to work and that that is why he is continuing the tradition of works of mercy. (It cannot be mere coincidence that the 'crime' of healing took place at the pool of Bethesda, which means 'House of Mercy'.) It was generally agreed among rabbis at this time that God must, in some sense, still be working even on the Sabbath and was therefore exempt from his own rule. In his reply to the 'Jews', Jesus indicates his equality with God, and his opponents are quick to note this (v. 18). Here we have a far more serious matter than the charge of Sabbath-breaking, that of blasphemy. Again we are in the realm of Christology. Who is Jesus? What is his relation to the Father? These were real issues for John and his church, as they would have been in the time of Jesus. They remain central for us today. In claiming a special relationship with the Father, was Jesus making himself 'equal with God' as the 'Jews' claim (v. 18)? Both Sabbath-breaking and blasphemy are capital offences. Jesus is on dangerous ground.

It is important to understand the usage John has for the term the 'Jews'. For many of us it sounds at the least politically incorrect and at worst anti-Semitic. What does John mean by this term, which will be increasingly used in this Gospel and which represents the enemies of God? Obviously, they are not ordinary Jews. We must remember that Jesus himself was a Jew, as were all his first disciples. For some reason John has chosen to limit his use of the word to the hostile Jewish authorities in Jerusalem. We can demonstrate this from this passage. The very fact that the paralytic is distinguished from the 'Jews' when he himself is very obviously a Jew suggests as much. Sadly, John's use of this term for hostile Jewish authorities has led to a lot of anti-

Semitism in the past. We can only speculate that so sharp was the dispute between Jews and Christians at the time of writing that John adopted the term as a pejorative description for those in opposition to the emerging Christian movement. We need to be aware that from now on in the text the term 'the Jews' represents the enemies of Jesus.

- **What is your attitude to the paralytic in this story? How do you think the first readers regarded him? Do you think he might represent a certain section of John's community who were still hanging back from making a decision about Jesus?**

- **Has John's pejorative use of the term the 'Jews' more to do with the difficulties of his first readers with their Jewish neighbours and their refusal to accept Jesus as the Messiah than to do with prejudice?**

- **Do you think that the New Testament treatment of Judaism led to more recent misunderstanding, hatred and even pogroms against the Jewish community?**

- **If so, what can Christians do to atone for this?**

- **The paralytic is presented as a member of 'the living dead' until his cure. Sadly, he failed to benefit fully from the offer of life. How true an assessment is this of us today?**

13

The Offer of Life

John 5.19–47

¹⁹Jesus gave them this answer: 'I tell you the truth, the Son can do nothing by himself; he can do only what he sees his Father doing, because whatever the Father does the Son also does. ²⁰For the Father loves the Son and shows him all he does. Yes, to your amazement he will show him even greater things than these. ²¹For just as the Father raises the dead and gives them life, even so the Son gives life to whom he is pleased to give it. ²²Moreover, the Father judges no-one, but has entrusted all judgment to the Son, ²³that all may honour the Son just as they honour the Father. He who does not honour the Son does not honour the Father, who sent him. ²⁴I tell you the truth, whoever hears my word and believes him who sent me has eternal life and will not be condemned; he has crossed over from death to life. ²⁵I tell you the truth, a time is coming and has now come when the dead will hear the voice of the Son of God and those who hear will live. ²⁶For as the Father has life in himself, so he has granted the Son to have life in himself. ²⁷And he has given him authority to judge because he is the Son of Man.

²⁸'Do not be amazed at this, for a time is coming when all who are in their graves will hear his voice ²⁹and come out—those who have done good will rise to live, and those who have done evil will rise to be condemned. ³⁰By myself I can do nothing; I judge only as I hear, and my judgment is just, for I seek not to please myself but him who sent me.

³¹'If I testify about myself, my testimony is not valid. ³²There is another who testifies in my favour, and I know that his testimony about me is valid.

³³'You have sent to John and he has testified to the truth. ³⁴Not that I accept human testimony; but I mention it that you may be saved. ³⁵John was a lamp that burned and gave light, and you chose for a time to enjoy his light.

³⁶'I have testimony weightier than that of John. For the very work that the Father has given me to finish, and which I am doing, testifies that the Father has sent me. ³⁷And the Father who sent me has himself testified concerning me. You have never heard his voice nor seen his form, ³⁸nor does his word dwell in you, for you do not believe the one he sent. ³⁹You diligently study the Scriptures because you think that by them you possess eternal life. These are the Scriptures that testify about me, ⁴⁰yet you refuse to come to me to have life.

⁴¹'I do not accept praise from men, ⁴²but I know you. I know that you do not have the

love of God in your hearts. ⁴³I have come in my Father's name, and you do not accept me; but if someone else comes in his own name, you will accept him. ⁴⁴How can you believe if you accept praise from one another, yet make no effort to obtain the praise that comes from the only God?

⁴⁵'But do not think I will accuse you before the Father. Your accuser is Moses, on whom your hopes are set. ⁴⁶If you believed Moses, you would believe me, for he wrote about me. ⁴⁷But since you do not believe what he wrote, how are you going to believe what I say?'

Jesus stands charged with the capital offence of blasphemy. In fact the scene is portrayed as a trial narrative with Jesus in the dock. A similar presentation can be found in second Isaiah (41.1–5, 21–9; 43.8–13; 44.6–8; 45.20–5), where the pagans are the antagonists and are judged to be false by God acting as the presiding judge who is also a party to the dispute.

The proverb 'like father like son' seems to lie behind Jesus' initial defence. 'Truly, truly, I say to you, the Son can do nothing of his own accord, but only what he sees the Father doing' (v. 19). The picture is that of a boy apprentice attached to his father from whom he learns his trade. If that is the basis for the relationship, then clearly the 'Jews' are misinterpreting what Jesus is saying. The difficulty arises when we examine the kind of work Jesus claims to be involved in, i.e. restoring life to the dead (v. 21) and participating in the final judgement of humankind (v. 24). What John's 'Jews' find objectionable is Jesus' claim to 'oneness' with God, that God is his Father in a special unique sense. Jesus' relationship with God is strongly emphasized in this Gospel, and the word 'Father' is constantly on the lips of Jesus. In fact it occurs fourteen times between verses 19 and 47. Jesus' defence is based on the claim that he and the Father are one, and the Father has given the Son authority in today's world and in God's future. The proof is to be found in the life-giving deeds of Jesus (vv. 21 and 24). Future hope has a present reality. The dead are hearing the voice of God in his Son. This is happening here and now (v. 25). This theme will be given pictorial expression in the story of the raising of Lazarus in chapter 11. At verse 30 there is a dramatic shift in the presentation. Jesus no longer talks in the third person of the 'Son' or the 'Son of Man'. Instead, he talks directly of himself in relation to the Father. Not only does this happen, but the defendant in this trial becomes the judge, although only in as much as he acts in concert with the Father's will (v. 30). Having made this claim, Jesus immediately cites a universal legal principle: one man's testimony accounts for nothing (v. 31). Presumably the first Christians had to deal with such an accusation when they proclaimed that Jesus said he was the Son of God. Like the other evangelists, John is keen to demonstrate the truth of who Jesus says he was. The first witness cited in defence of this claim is John the Baptist (vv. 33–5). If the evidence of the deeds will not convince Jesus' accusers then the testimony of the Baptist is offered as universally respected witness. Yet this does not compare with that of God, which shines through the deeds of Jesus (v. 36). The evidence is there for those with eyes to see and ears to hear. Sadly, his accusers are both blind and deaf (v. 37). They do not have the 'Word' abiding in them to interpret the events as God-given. Indeed their reading of Scripture is defective and veiled. Paul makes a similar complaint in 2 Corinthians (3.14–15). The problem for John is that some have accepted the 'Word' made flesh while others sit on the fence like Nicodemus or reject the 'Word' like the 'Jews' in this passage. 'He came to his own and his own received him not'(1.11). 'I have come in my Father's name and you do not receive me'(v. 43). In refusing him Jesus' opponents condemn themselves; in accepting him they accept life with God, and pass from death to life (v. 24).

- **Is the defence that Jesus offers convincing or does it only make sense to those who accept his claim to be the Son of God in a unique sense?**

- **Jesus' relationship with God makes life-enhancing grace available to those who believe in Jesus. Can you put this in some other words?**

- **Why is Christology so important to John?**

14

The Fourth Sign:
A Free Lunch for Five Thousand

John 6.1–15

¹**Some time after this, Jesus crossed to the** far shore of the Sea of Galilee (that is, the Sea of Tiberias), ²and a great crowd of people followed him because they saw the miraculous signs he had performed on the sick. ³Then Jesus went up on a mountainside and sat down with his disciples. ⁴The Jewish Passover Feast was near.

⁵When Jesus looked up and saw a great crowd coming towards him, he said to Philip, 'Where shall we buy bread for these people to eat?' ⁶He asked this only to test him, for he already had in mind what he was going to do.

⁷Philip answered him, 'Eight months' wages would not buy enough bread for each one to have a bite!'

⁸Another of his disciples, Andrew, Simon Peter's brother, spoke up, ⁹'Here is a boy with five small barley loaves and two small fish, but how far will they go among so many?'

¹⁰Jesus said, 'Make the people sit down.' There was plenty of grass in that place, and the men sat down, about five thousand of them. ¹¹Jesus then took the loaves, gave thanks, and distributed to those who were seated as much as they wanted. He did the same with the fish.

¹²When they had all had enough to eat, he said to his disciples, 'Gather the pieces that are left over. Let nothing be wasted.' ¹³So they gathered them and filled twelve baskets with the pieces of the five barley loaves left over by those who had eaten.

¹⁴After the people saw the miraculous sign that Jesus did, they began to say, 'Surely this is the Prophet who is to come into the world.' ¹⁵Jesus, knowing that they intended to come and make him king by force, withdrew again to a mountain by himself.

Chapter 5 ended with a complaint that the Jews had failed to understand their own lawgiver, Moses. This chapter will attempt to demonstrate the extent of that failure. We shall look at a number of allusions to the Exodus story of which Moses was the hero. Indeed some scholars have seen Moses lurking behind chapter 7 and chapter 8 (with reference to living water and the Light of the World). In as much as Moses is identified with the old dispensation, it is difficult not to see references to him. The prologue has testified that only the law came through

Moses, while 'grace and truth came through Jesus Christ' (1.18).

The chapter opens by setting the scene. Jesus crosses the lake at Passover time followed by crowds. Already there are echoes with the other Gospels, for instance, in such phrases as 'the other side' of the lake. There is a hint here of the 'Galilean spring time' that we are familiar with in the other Gospels. Sadly, this will not last. Sitting down among the hills with his disciples Jesus is portrayed as in Matthew's Gospel as a new Moses about to deliver a new law. John hints at his own concerns, though. Like the Jews of chapter 2 (v. 23) the Galilean crowds are following Jesus for the wrong reasons, and this will be developed throughout the chapter.

The story of the miraculous feeding is the most often told in the Gospels. John narrates the story beautifully, with plenty of dialogue and attention to detail. Jesus tests the disciples' faith in him by asking them how the people are to be fed. As with everything in this Gospel, there are two levels of understanding. Here it depends on the faith and perception of the one being questioned. In this case Philip answers. Making some quick calculations, he estimates the cost is well beyond their means, even if there was a village shop or market nearby. Andrew, the great enabler of this Gospel, shows more understanding of the possibilities of the situation by introducing the lad with a packed lunch of barley bread (associated with the poor) and dried fish. However, even he is sceptical. Contrast this with the faith of the young lad. He is the only character in the story who trusts Jesus implicitly. He can see clearly that Jesus can make good use of his meagre gift. His action is an illustration of what Jesus has to say in the synoptic Gospels about the faith of little children (Mark 10.15). Nevertheless, the offer is enough to trigger the most important sign so far. Jesus retains the initiative, inviting the large numbers of men to sit (or perhaps recline, as the twelve will do at the Last Supper). What follows has been variously described as a messianic banquet, the great marriage supper of the Lamb (Revelation 19.6–9), or a foretaste of the Last Supper. Whatever interpretation is decided on the meal reflects something of the Passover experience that the passage has already alluded to (v. 4). Are these men fed miraculously as their forefathers were by Moses? Are they now called into a new covenant relationship sealed in the eucharistic allusions of thanking (v. 23), taking, breaking and distributing. What is certain is the concern that nothing be lost (v. 12). One of the works of the Son commissioned by the Father is the safe gathering in of all that is entrusted to him (6.39; cf. 17.12). The disciples entrusted with this task may come to see their actions in terms of their role in gathering 'into one the children of God who are scattered abroad' (11.52).

This notable miracle is met with a popular response (vv. 14–15). That Jesus is a prophet is the reported response of the crowd as described in the synoptics (Mark 8.28 and parallels). However, John deliberately describes Jesus as the Prophet, which is the designation of Moses in Deuteronomy 18.15 ff. and the like of which God promised to raise up. The last verse in this passage is very significant for our understanding of Jesus. It is reported that the crowd, once they began to realize that Jesus was the Prophet like Moses, wanted to make him their king. It was for this reason that Jesus had to withdraw. It is well known that the hills around Galilee harboured a number of Zealot garrisons. It may be that we have here an attempt by the Zealot community to elect Jesus as their leader. We know that Jesus had at least one Zealot among the Twelve, that he was crucified between two possible Zealots and that the superscription on the cross declared the charge 'the king of the Jews'. There appears to be a real reticence on Jesus' part to be identified with a political cause. His kingdom is not of this world.

- **What is this miracle a sign of? It has been seen as**
  a) a sign of God at work in Jesus;
  b) a signal that the new age has begun in which God will provide for his people;
  c) a demonstration of his prodigal provision towards those who put their trust in him.

- **Do the disciples in the story represent our cautious conditional faith?**

- **If the people see Jesus as this Prophet, are they coming to an understanding of who he is?**

- **Do people on the edge of the Church see him in these terms today?**

15

Crossing the Lake

John 6.16–24

16When evening came, his disciples went down to the lake, 17where they got into a boat and set off across the lake for Capernaum. By now it was dark, and Jesus had not yet joined them. 18A strong wind was blowing and the waters grew rough. 19When they had rowed three or three and a half miles, they saw Jesus approaching the boat, walking on the water; and they were terrified. 20But he said to them, 'It is I; don't be afraid.' 21Then they were willing to take him into the boat, and immediately the boat reached the shore where they were heading.

22The next day the crowd that had stayed on the opposite shore of the lake realised that only one boat had been there, and that Jesus had not entered it with his disciples, but that they had gone away alone. 23Then some boats from Tiberias landed near the place where the people had eaten the bread after the Lord had given thanks. 24Once the crowd realised that neither Jesus nor his disciples were there, they got into the boats and went to Capernaum in search of Jesus.

A version of this strange story can be found in two of the other Gospels (Mark 6.45–52 and Matthew 14.22–33). They are remarkably similar in content and in the use to which they are put, emphasizing the divine power working through Jesus and its effects over wind and wave, 'his path through the great waters' (Psalm 77.19). John, as we might expect, makes a little more of the story. In his version there is more emphasis on the reference to the divine name 'I am' (v. 20). Jesus is revealing more of his intimate relation to the Father. He uses the same form of words to the Samaritan woman, but from now on Jesus will use the term more openly with his disciples in an attempt to instruct them in the characteristics of the relationship with the Father into which they are being inducted. In this case, he that has satisfied the hunger of his people in the desert is now rescuing them from the terrors of the watery depths. Again the parallels with Moses are obvious. However, one greater than Moses is here to save them from harm and to confirm their understanding of who it is who offers such salvation. They need not fear. Once they take Jesus 'on board', their anxieties are put to rest and they immediately reach their destination. In this brief story all the elemental fears that beset humankind are overcome. The chaos of darkness and the watery abyss which are described in the first chapter of Genesis are overcome by the one who was in the beginning with God. The Word of God, first expressed at the creation, is active and real in the world and being experienced by those who put their trust in him.

Those who have only partially understood who Jesus is and what he represents are not included in this epiphany of Jesus to his disciples. They are left on the other side of the lake seeking the real Jesus. So far they have misunderstood his mission. This is the reason why they are left behind. What the disciples experience in the boat may be an illustration of what the newly baptized member of John's church might have undergone: the sense of being adrift in a chaotic and hostile world, the reassurance in finding a Christ who calls out to them in their distress, the experience of oneness with a saving God and the acceptance of him as saviour with the resultant joy and sense of safety experienced. All this is apparent in this passage and must have been a source of encouragement to those who were making sense of their new life in the community of faith. For those in the community who have not made this faith commitment they, like the crowd in this chapter, must go on seeking an elusive Christ who from now on will seem to play a game of hide and seek with them. The crowd have not yet understood the significance of the feeding miracle. That is why John has them remaining at the site where the event took place. They have not moved on from the merely material interpretation of the miracle. For them it is an occasion for free food and an opportunity to enlist this new prophet to lead them out of slavery as Moses did.

Verse 24 presents us with an almost comic scene of the crowd running about desperately seeking Jesus. They manage to flag down a fleet of passing boats from Tiberias, commandeering them to take them (all five thousand plus those already on the Tiberias boats!?) to Capernaum, where they continue the search. The theme of seeking Jesus is common in John's Gospel. In chapter 12 there is an important moment when some Greeks come seeking him. The most famous seeking scene is that in the Easter garden when the risen Christ asks the weeping Magdelene whom she seeks.

Nowhere in John is the miraculous nature of these events discussed. It is not an issue for him. Living in a pre-scientific age, these stories were credible to his contemporaries in a way they are not to a later generation. What is of immense interest to him is how these events are interpreted. What they mean to him and his readers, and how they inform and encourage their faith, is his main concern. For as he says himself, 'these signs are written that you may believe that Jesus is the Christ, the Son of God, and that believing you may have life in his name' (20.31).

- Do you think we should we be bothered less about the historical facts and more about the interpretation and meaning of these stories?

- Does this story inform and encourage our faith in 'Jesus as the Christ, the Son of God'? What do these terms mean for us today?

- Mark defines discipleship in terms of being with Jesus. Does John's Gospel confirm or modify that view?

- How important is it for us to continue John's emphasis on the quest for a true understanding of who Jesus is?

REACTIONS TAKE PLACE

16

The Bread of Life: The Reaction of the Crowd

John 6.25–40

[25]**When they found him on the other side** of the lake, they asked him, 'Rabbi, when did you get here?'
[26]Jesus answered, 'I tell you the truth, you are looking for me, not because you saw miraculous signs but because you ate the loaves and had your fill. [27]Do not work for food that spoils, but for food that endures to eternal life, which the Son of Man will give you. On him God the Father has placed his seal of approval.'
[28]Then they asked him, 'What must we do to do the works God requires?'
[29]Jesus answered, 'The work of God is this: to believe in the one he has sent.'
[30]So they asked him, 'What miraculous sign then will you give that we may see it and believe you? What will you do? [31]Our forefathers ate the manna in the desert; as it is written: "He gave them bread from heaven to eat."'
[32]Jesus said to them, 'I tell you the truth, it is not Moses who has given you the bread from heaven, but it is my Father who gives you the true bread from heaven. [33]For the bread of God is he who comes down from heaven and gives life to the world.'
[34]"Sir,' they said, 'from now on give us this bread.'
[35]Then Jesus declared, 'I am the bread of life. He who comes to me will never go hungry, and he who believes in me will never be thirsty. [36]But as I told you, you have seen me and still you do not believe. [37]All that the Father gives me will come to me, and whoever comes to me I will never drive away. [38]For I have come down from heaven not to do my will but to do the will of him who sent me. [39]And this is the will of him who sent me, that I shall lose none of all that he has given me, but raise them up at the last day. [40]For my Father's will is that everyone who looks to the Son and believes in him shall have eternal life, and I will raise him up at the last day.'

The crowd catch up with their quarry. Jesus is discovered in the synagogue at Capernaum. These astonished seekers (numbering several thousand, John has not indicated otherwise) are more concerned to discover how Jesus got there than to continue to learn from his teaching. Jesus ignores their shallow question and criticizes them for their lack of perception. They should not seek a free lunch but concentrate on the spiritual food that endures to eternal life (v. 27). The fact that this saying is introduced with the solemn wording 'I tell you the truth' suggests that it be taken seriously. It should not be imagined that anything in John is not serious in intention, but some sayings are meant to have greater impact than others, and this is a case in point. Jesus is warning the Galilean masses of the spiritual dimension to life that they seem to overlook. Again John is alluding to the synoptic tradition in which Jesus warns that we cannot live by bread alone and that our prayer should be for daily bread of a spiritual nature. The source and origin of this bread will be the concern of the rest of this chapter.

Up until now Jesus has been elusive with the crowd. He now enters a dialogue with them which, it has to be admitted, is equally elusive. Interaction and understanding are possible, but only if his hearers will allow their imaginations to include the spiritual dimension that Jesus prefers to work with. From now on Jesus will talk of spiritual realities in the language of heaven. Like the dialogue with the woman of Samaria, it is possible for the hearers to understand but only if they accept the heavenly origin of the words they hear. For instance it was not Moses that gave the bread in the desert but God (v. 32). As Matthew and Luke emphasize in the story of the temptation of Jesus (Matthew 4.1–11; Luke 4.1–14), it is 'not by bread alone' that they should live 'but by the word of God'. That word is now addressing them in a language they can understand, if and only if they recognize its origin and authority. All that is required is that they, who have come on a quest seeking Jesus, come to him with their spiritual hunger which he claims he will satisfy (vv. 35–6). Like the woman at the well who heard Jesus talk of heavenly water, the crowd ask for a constant supply of 'bread from heaven' (v. 34).

The only way to earn this bread from heaven is for them to believe in Jesus as the very 'bread of life' (v. 35). 'I am the bread of life; he who comes to me shall not hunger, and he shall not thirst.' Sadly, it seems that some of the crowd cannot accept this (v. 36). Here we have yet another development of the theme, 'he came to his own and his own received him not' (1.12). But those who do receive this message will be sustained to eternal life (v. 40). In some ways this section of John's Gospel is the equivalent of the rejection scene found in Mark 6. Again we have Jesus in a Galilean synagogue initially welcomed as a prophet only to be rejected by his own people.

- It is clear that for John's Gospel a full understanding of who Jesus is and what he represents is essential as a prerequisite to discipleship. How important is it for us to have an understanding of the nature and person of Jesus?

- Is the Jesus of John making too many demands on our faith?

- In the words of the Galilean crowd, 'What must we do, to be doing the works of God?'

- What are today's crowds seeking?

17

The Bread of Life: The Reaction of the 'Jews'

John 6.41–59

⁴¹**At this the Jews began to grumble about** him because he said, 'I am the bread that came down from heaven.' ⁴²They said, 'Is this not Jesus, the son of Joseph, whose father and mother we know? How can he now say, "I came down from heaven"?' ⁴³'Stop grumbling among yourselves,' Jesus answered. ⁴⁴"No-one can come to me unless the Father who sent me draws him, and I will raise him up at the last day. ⁴⁵It is written in the Prophets: "They will all be taught by God." Everyone who listens to the Father and learns from him comes to me. ⁴⁶No-one has seen the Father except the one who is from God; only he has seen the Father. ⁴⁷I tell you the truth, he who believes has everlasting life. ⁴⁸I am the bread of life. ⁴⁹Your forefathers ate the manna in the desert, yet they died. ⁵⁰But here is the bread that comes down from heaven, which a man may eat and not die. ⁵¹I am the living bread that came down from heaven. If anyone eats of this bread, he will live for ever. This bread is my flesh, which I will give for the life of the world.'

⁵²Then the Jews began to argue sharply among themselves, 'How can this man give us his flesh to eat?'

⁵³Jesus said to them, 'I tell you the truth, unless you can eat the flesh of the Son of Man and drink his blood, you have no life in you. ⁵⁴Whoever eats my flesh and drinks my blood has eternal life, and I will raise him up at the last day. ⁵⁵For my flesh is real food and my blood is real drink. ⁵⁶Whoever eats my flesh and drinks my blood remains in me, and I in him. ⁵⁷Just as the living Father sent me and I live because of the Father, so the one who feeds on me will live because of me. ⁵⁸This is the bread that came down from heaven. Your forefathers ate manna and died, but he who feeds on this bread will live for ever.' ⁵⁹He said this while teaching in the synagogue in Capernaum.

The audience suddenly changes. No longer are we dealing with the wandering crowds that pursued Jesus from the site of the feeding miracle. We are now confronted with an audience of hostile 'murmuring' Jews. Again John seems insensitive to the fact that all his characters, with the exception of the Roman official, are 'Jews'. But as we have noted, by 'Jews' John means the religious leadership determined to destroy Jesus. By implication they were still causing the original readers of this Gospel difficulties.

The murmuring occurs in all four Gospels and is particularly destructive. Jesus is usually aware of it and confronts it as in the text here. Like the situation in the Nazareth synagogue as recorded in Mark 6, the problem is to do with origins. How can a 'local lad' make such claims for himself? The 'Jews' in this dialogue talk of genealogies. It is interesting to note that Matthew and Luke both feel the need to deal with this issue at the beginning of their Gospels, while Mark and John ignore the problem. For both of them their Jesus needs no credentials or pedigree, his authority is from God. The discussion which follows represents a dialogue of the deaf. Both parties talk on separate levels. It is as if they are using separate languages. The 'Jews' pick up a subtle shift in the language that Jesus is using. Up until this point Jesus has talked in terms of being the provider of the spiritual bread in question. He has now identified himself as that bread. The feeder becomes the food which has come down from heaven. This is precisely the issue raging between Jews and Christians and is the central argument of this Gospel. This 'incarnation' doctrine was and is unacceptable to Judaism, and the solemn reinstatement of it in verses 47–51 does nothing to persuade them.

The dialogue widens in that the issues that Jesus discusses can only further alienate his audience. There is an implied contrast with the figure of Moses, who supplied perishable bread in the wilderness to perishable Israelites (v. 48): 'Your fathers ate bread in the wilderness, and they died'. The bread Jesus offers guarantees against death, those who eat of it 'will live forever' (v. 51). Moreover this bread that Jesus offers is identified with his own flesh (v. 51). If there is a dispute as to the veracity of this doctrine then it is authenticated not from the books of Moses but from the prophets who testify that 'they shall be taught by God' (v. 45). The only one who has seen the Father, Jesus says, is 'he who comes from God' (v. 46). It is very obvious to the reader that this person is none other than Jesus himself, and this was clearly stated in the prologue (1.18). The discussion comes to a climax when it is quite clear that Jesus is not being compared to Moses but to God. Amazingly, the 'Jews' do not seem to pick up this point and do not level a charge of blasphemy. Instead what they are concerned about is the language about eating his flesh. Jesus concludes the discussion with what appears to be eucharistic language (vv. 53–8), but may in fact be a pointer to his death, in which the disciple is expected to participate in order to bring life to the world.

- John's Gospel contains a full description of the Last Supper, but no account of the institution of the eucharistic meal. Is this section a presentation of his eucharistic theology?

- Is the language of eating the flesh and blood of Jesus as repulsive to you as it was to the 'Jews' in this passage? If it is, does this bother you? If not, should it?

- What does Jesus mean when he says 'He who eats my flesh and drinks my blood has eternal life, and I shall raise him up at the last day'?

18

The Reaction of the Disciples

John 6.60–71

⁶⁰**On hearing it, many of his disciples said,** 'This is a hard teaching. Who can accept it?' ⁶¹Aware that his disciples were grumbling about this, Jesus said to them, 'Does this offend you? ⁶²What if you see the Son of Man ascend to where he was before! ⁶³The Spirit gives life; the flesh counts for nothing. The words I have spoken to you are spirit and they are life. ⁶⁴Yet there are some of you who do not believe.' For Jesus had known from the beginning which of them did not believe and who would betray him. ⁶⁵He went on to say, 'This is why I told you that no-one can come to me unless the Father has enabled him.'

⁶⁶From this time many of his disciples turned back and no longer followed him. ⁶⁷'You do not want to leave too, do you?' Jesus asked the Twelve. ⁶⁸Simon Peter answered him, 'Lord, to whom shall we go? You have the words of eternal life. ⁶⁹We believe and know that you are the Holy One of God.' ⁷⁰Then Jesus replied, 'Have I not chosen you, the Twelve? Yet one of you is a devil!' ⁷¹(He meant Judas, the son of Simon Iscariot, who, though one of the Twelve, was later to betray him.)

If the Galilean crowd and the 'Jews' had difficulty in accepting what Jesus was saying, we should not be surprised if the disciples appear to baulk at this 'hard saying' (v. 60). The saying is not hard for them to understand. But it is hard to accept this talk about sharing in the flesh and blood sacrifice that Jesus has indicated as a pre-condition for discipleship. As with Peter in Mark 8, all this seems too much to take. The disciples had not bargained on this sort of messiah, one that would sacrifice himself totally in the service of the Father and expect as much from them. Perhaps this demand is put more graphically in the instruction to take up our crosses and follow Jesus (Matthew 16.24; Mark 8.34; 10.21; Luke 9.23).

The call to sacrificial self-giving is given a different slant in John's Gospel. The community for whom this was written had begun to suffer persecution at the instigation of the Jewish authorities, and some had probably been expelled from the synagogues. It was important for them to see that this suffering was part of what Jesus expected from them; indeed, it was a way for them to identify with the experience of their Lord and Master. More than that, all this was a way of cementing that solidarity, that total union with the Father and each other, which is the hallmark of the Christian as one who abides in Christ.

This interpretation is given support in the saying about the 'going up' of the Son of Man. The Son of Man is an eschatological figure taken from Daniel 7 and associated with the end-time. In the book of Daniel the saints of God, the righteous remnant, are persecuted by the beasts representing the world powers. However, the 'Ancient of Days' vindicates and rescues them in the form of a corporate Son of Man figure who helps usher in the reign of God and his saints. All the Gospels are unanimous in presenting a Jesus who prefers to describe himself as the Son of Man. This self-designation of Jesus is one that exactly fits the experience of many of the first Christians, especially those in John's church community. In this passage Jesus adopts the language of the Son of Man in order to allude to his sacrificial role. The same term is used in the other Gospels when Jesus speaks of his passion and resurrection, and the same fearful and puzzled response is found in his disciples (Mark 8.31, 9.31,10.33 and parallels). Here he talks of them taking offence and leads them on to consider the even more offensive suggestion of his 'going up' to where he was before. The phrase is deliberately ambiguous and can mean elevated to glory or going up to Jerusalem (a place Jesus has already visited in this Gospel) to be lifted up on the cross. John makes considerable play on spatial imagery and the language of elevation. For him ascension is achieved by reigning in glory from his throne on the cross, the place from which he will bequeath his spirit. As a man of spirit he can and will convey the words of eternal life. The Baptist foretold this, and it will become even more apparent at his glorification (7.18). For now, Jesus acknowledges that many of the Galilean disciples were unable to follow him, and he is aware that a disciple will betray him (v. 64). Indeed, John ends the chapter by identifying the betrayer as Judas. Although many draw back, the twelve pledge their conviction that in coming to Jesus they have experienced the quickening words of eternal life. As in Mark 8, Peter speaks on behalf of the twelve. In this passage his identification of Jesus as the 'Holy One of God' (v. 69) is not as direct as that found in Mark ('You are the Christ' – Mark 8.29), but he does recognize in Jesus 'the words of eternal life' (v. 68).

- Is John placing a changed emphasis on the disciples' understanding of Jesus?

- Notice the title Peter uses, 'the Holy One of God'. It is the same as that used by the demons in Mark's account of Jesus exorcizing. Are the disciples motivated by fear of being cast off from Jesus?

- Notice how Jesus accuses one of the twelve of being a devil (v. 70). How secure is our faith? Do we take too much for granted? In what way would we be likely to 'betray' Jesus?

19

The Family's Reaction to Jesus: The Journey to Jerusalem

John 7.1–13

¹**After this, Jesus went around in Galilee,** purposely staying away from Judea because the Jews there were waiting to take his life. ²But when the Jewish Feast of Tabernacles was near, ³Jesus' brothers said to him, 'You ought to leave here and go to Judea, so that your disciples may see the miracles you do. ⁴No-one who wants to become a public figure acts in secret. Since you are doing these things, show yourself to the world.' ⁵For even his own brothers did not believe in him. ⁶Therefore Jesus told them, 'The right time for me has not yet come; for you any time is right. ⁷The world cannot hate you, but it hates me because I testify that what it does is evil.

⁸You go to the Feast. I am not yet going up to this Feast, because for me the right time has not yet come.' ⁹Having said this, he stayed in Galilee.

¹⁰However, after his brothers had left for the Feast, he went also, not publicly, but in secret. ¹¹Now at the Feast the Jews were watching for him and asking, 'Where is that man?' ¹²Among the crowds there was widespread whispering about him. Some said, 'He is a good man.'

Others replied, 'No, he deceives the people.' ¹³But no-one would say anything publicly about him for fear of the Jews.

The first verse of this new section of the Gospel tells us that Jesus undertook a peripatetic ministry around Galilee like that more fully described in the other Gospels. It forms no part of John's purpose to describe this ministry of teaching and healing. He indicates a knowledge of these doings at the end of his Gospel (21.25). This verse alludes to that knowledge, but John now restricts himself to the reaction that Jesus precipitates among his countrymen. John again indicates his understanding of the term 'the Jews' by locating them in Judea, rather than in Galilee. It is the religious authorities who seek his demise, and that can only be achieved at Jerusalem when the time is right.

The time may not be ripe, but the hour is drawing ever nearer. Another feast is at hand. This time it is the popular feast of Tabernacles, which takes place after the harvest and before the new year festival. This is a good time for the evangelist to indicate a new change in direction. The prologue has referred to the Word 'tenting' or 'tabernacling' with his people (1.14). This feast, in which Jewish families made themselves little leafy booths to recall their time in the wilderness when they received the law, provides an opportunity for Jesus to demonstrate this truth to those who will receive it.

It is implied from this passage that the brothers of Jesus did not accept him. However, they urge a course of action that some political 'spin doctor' might advocate today to a politician whose popularity is waning. They tell him not to waste his time in the provinces but to go up to Jerusalem where all the action is, especially as it is holiday time. The crowd will be looking for some diversion, and Jesus might find himself a big break. We are reminded again of the picture John paints of the mother of Jesus who urges him to make something of a splash at the Cana wedding. As then, Jesus is reluctant to act on such advice: his 'time has not yet come' (v. 6). Jesus prefers to act privately. He sets off for his third visit to Jerusalem. It will be just as controversial as the other two visits and will prove to be his last. From now on the pace slows down, but the action intensifies. Jesus has come to his own, but his own accept him not. He is a light shining in the darkness, but the darkness will try to overcome that light (John 1.11, 5).

The elusive Jesus will be a continuing theme from now on. As the brothers predicted, Jesus is expected by the 'Jews' of Jerusalem. The 'muttering' we met in chapter 6 is still prevalent (v. 12), and we learn later that opinion is still divided (v. 43).

- **What considerations might have led Jesus to change his mind and go up to Jerusalem?**

- **Is it possible that Jesus was deliberately deceiving his family?**

- **How significant is it that Jesus seems unable to secure the support of his own family?**

20

Jesus Comes Out into the Open

John 7.14–36

¹⁴**Not until halfway through the Feast did** Jesus go up to the temple courts and begin to teach. ¹⁵The Jews were amazed and asked, 'How did this man get such learning without having studied?'

¹⁶Jesus answered, 'My teaching is not my own. It comes from him who sent me. ¹⁷If anyone chooses to do God's will, he will find out whether my teaching comes from God or whether I speak on my own. ¹⁸He who speaks on his own does so to gain honour for himself, but he who works for the honour of the one who sent him is a man of truth; there is nothing false about him. ¹⁹Has not Moses given you the law? Yet not one of you keeps the law. Why are you trying to kill me?'

²⁰'You are demon-possessed,' the crowd answered. 'Who is trying to kill you?'

²¹Jesus said to them, 'I did one miracle, and you are all astonished. ²²Yet, because Moses gave you circumcision (though actually it did not come from Moses, but from the patriarchs), you circumcise a child on the Sabbath. ²³Now if a child can be circumcised on the Sabbath so that the law of Moses may not be broken, why are you angry with me for healing the whole man on the Sabbath? ²⁴Stop judging by mere appearances, and make a right judgment.'

²⁵At that point some of the people of Jerusalem began to ask, 'Isn't this the man they are trying to kill? ²⁶Here he is, speaking publicly, and they are not saying a word to him. Have the authorities really concluded that he is the Christ? ²⁷But we know where this man is from; when the Christ comes, no-one will know where he is from.'

²⁸Then Jesus, still teaching in the temple courts, cried out, 'Yes, you know me, and you know where I am from. I am not here on my own, but he who sent me is true. You do not know him, ²⁹but I know him because I am from him and he sent me.'

³⁰At this they tried to seize him, but no-one laid a hand on him, because his time had not yet come. ³¹Still, many in the crowd put their faith in him. They said, 'When the Christ comes, will he do more miraculous signs than this man?'

³²The Pharisees heard the crowd whispering such things about him. Then the chief priests and the Pharisees sent temple guards to arrest him.

³³Jesus said, 'I am with you for only a short time, and then I go to the one who sent me. ³⁴You will look for me, but you will not find me; and where I am, you cannot come.'

³⁵The Jews said to one another, 'Where does this man intend to go that we cannot find him? Will he go where our people live scattered

among the Greeks, and teach the Greeks? | look for me, but you will not find me," and
[36]What did he mean when he said, "You will | "Where I am, you cannot come"?'

If Jesus is to make a debut then he could not have chosen a more prominent location. The other Gospels place his first attempt at public preaching in the local synagogue at Nazareth, where he received a very mixed reception. Here things are not much better. However, this time the interchange between teacher and listeners is more extended. In fact here we find the familiar 'trial' language that we noticed in chapter 6. Another factor common to all four Gospels is the initial reaction of the crowds when first hearing Jesus. They all marvel to hear such teaching (Mark 1.22, 6.2; Matthew 7.28, 29; 13.54; Luke 4.22, 32). What was the cause of such astonishment? The answer is, in one word, 'authority'. Jesus taught with such a charismatic authority that many were drawn to him while others muttered about credentials and sound learning. Here we see the issue developed in terms of a debate about origins. Not only is there a dispute about from where Jesus gets his authorization, there is also the question about where he comes from.

The 'Jews' and the Pharisees in this chapter are set on misunderstanding and perverting what Jesus has to say. The crowd are presented in a slightly more ambivalent light, some speculating that he might be the 'Christ' (v. 26) while others accuse him of having a 'demon' (v. 20). They seem incapable of coming to any firm conclusion because they are described as being 'afraid of the Jews'.

Maybe we have here yet another glimpse into the world in which John's Gospel first appeared. If the Christian Church is breaking away from its Jewish roots, then these are precisely the kinds of issues which would be concerning the readers of this Gospel. Part of the test as to the authenticity of Jesus and his radical teaching lay in an assessment of his credentials. For those convinced of his divine origins then there was no argument, but for the undecided there was everything to play for.

The trauma caused by the fall of Jerusalem in AD 70 must have been comparable to that experienced at the Exile some eight centuries earlier. Most Jews were removed from their heartland. The temple was no more and they were forced to regroup and redefine their faith. What they regarded as a heretical Christian sect had a reputation for being critical of the temple, and its leader had even talked of its destruction and replacement. He was remembered for his free interpretation of the law and his radical attitude to the Sabbath. The debate we are witnessing in this chapter touches on most of these points at issue, including the suggestion that Jesus might proselytize the gentiles (v. 35). The only solution that the beleaguered authorities can come up with is to have this Jesus removed. This plot is known to the crowd (v. 25) and to Jesus himself (v. 19). Indeed, the Pharisees put their plan into action by instructing the guard to arrest him (v. 32), but without success; as we hear later even the soldiery are affected by his charisma (v. 46).

- How do you recognize authoritative teaching today?

- Is it the fear of what others might say or think that restricts people in making up their own minds about issues of importance?

- Has there always been a history of intimidation that has threatened our freedom of choice?

- Do you think Jesus can liberate people from this kind of fear of intimidation? What risks are involved in speaking openly about one's doubts or convictions?

THE LIGHT SHINES THROUGH

21

Where Does He Come From?

John 7.37–52

³⁷**On the last and greatest day of the Feast,** Jesus stood and said in a loud voice, 'If anyone is thirsty, let him come to me and drink. ³⁸Whoever believes in me, as the Scripture has said, streams of living water will flow from within him.' ³⁹By this he meant the Spirit, whom those who believed in him were later to receive. Up to that time the Spirit had not been given, since Jesus had not yet been glorified.

⁴⁰On hearing his words, some of the people said, 'Surely this man is the Prophet.'

⁴¹Others said, 'He is the Christ'

Still others asked, 'How can the Christ come from Galilee? ⁴²Does not the Scripture say that the Christ will come from David's family and from Bethlehem, the town where David lived?' ⁴³Thus the people were divided because of Jesus. ⁴⁴Some wanted to seize him, but no-one laid a hand on him.

⁴⁵Finally the temple guards went back to the chief priests and Pharisees, who asked them, 'Why didn't you bring him in?'

⁴⁶'No-one ever spoke the way this man does,' the guards declared.

⁴⁷'You mean he has deceived you also?' the Pharisees retorted. ⁴⁸'Has any of the rulers or of the Pharisees believed in him? ⁴⁹No! But this mob that knows nothing of the law— there is a curse on them.'

⁵⁰Nicodemus, who had gone to Jesus earlier and who was one of their own number, asked, ⁵¹'Does our law condemn a man without first hearing him to find out what he is doing?'

⁵²They replied, 'Are you from Galilee, too? Look into it, and you will find that a prophet does not come out of Galilee.'

In the area now known as Silwan in East Jerusalem there is the ancient spring of Gihon which is the reason for Jerusalem's existence. Without this water supply the city would never have been built in such an inaccessible spot. The water is directed from here by means of an ancient tunnel into the old city and is collected at the pool of Siloam. Three thousand years ago David took the city from the Jebusites by means of this tunnel. His son Solomon was proclaimed king at this spring. Now Jesus, as the Davidic successor, makes a claim to be the source of living water. This statement is made on the feast day when water is taken from this spring and poured on the altar in the temple. In a very few verses John has made a number of references to important Jewish traditions (kingship, the temple, salvation), and Jesus is seen to be the new source of all these concepts. He is the unproclaimed messiah king who will liberate and lead his people. Like David and Solomon he will lead his people and give them new hope and purpose. As the source of living water he offers to sustain them with God's renewing spirit. To help drive home the message, the evangelist explains that the water he is referring to is the Spirit which is now available to all believers because Jesus is glorified (v. 39).

This stimulates some speculation among the bystanders. Here we have an even more complex pattern of division: some are ready to accept Jesus as the Christ; others remain as sceptical as Nathanael about Jesus' origins. Galilee is not a contender as far as the Pharisees are concerned, and they seek to have this 'pretender' removed. Nicodemus, who we met by night in chapter 3, almost comes to the rescue. I say 'almost' because Nicodemus has not quite come out into the open, but as a vocal member of the Jewish Council he does speak up for common justice, insisting on Jesus having the benefit of a fair trial. What is also significant is that Nicodemus is interested in hearing what Jesus does (v. 51). His fellow Council members are quick to see the significance of this remark. They accuse him of being a Galilean in the same way as the temple servants accuse Peter of being from Galilee during the very trial that Nicodemus is here pleading for.

The Spirit of which Jesus speaks in this passage is related to water as it was in the discussion with Nicodemus (3.5) and in chapter 4 when Jesus talks with the Samaritan woman about water welling up into eternal life. God, whom Jesus defines as 'Spirit' in that passage (4.24), is the source of this life-giving power which will be freely available to all those who enter into the suffering life and death of Jesus. Jesus will give up his Spirit to the Father as he dies on the cross. He will receive it back again at the resurrection and breathe it into his disciples as a life-enhancing force at their commissioning on the first Easter Day (20.22). The allusion to the baptismal rite is never far from the surface in these discussions.

- **Why do you think there was suspicion among the Pharisees about Galilee?**

- **What part is Nicodemus playing in this drama?**

- **Does the reference to water in the temple confines remind you of other references to water in Ezekiel? Try and find the passage and discuss its meaning in connection with what you have read in John.**

- **John ignores the tradition that the Messiah is to be born in Bethlehem – why do you think this is so?**

22

The Woman Taken in Adultery

John 7.53—8.11

53Then each went to his own home.
8:1But Jesus went to the Mount of Olives. 2At dawn he appeared again in the temple courts, where all the people gathered round him, and he sat down to teach them. 3The teachers of the law and the Pharisees brought in a woman caught in adultery. They made her stand before the group 4and said to Jesus, 'Teacher, this woman was caught in the act of adultery. 5In the Law Moses commanded us to stone such women. Now what do you say?' 6They were using this question as a trap, in order to have a basis for accusing him.
But Jesus bent down and started to write on the ground with his finger. 7When they kept on questioning him, he straightened up and said to them, 'If any one of you is without sin, let him be the first to throw a stone at her.' 8Again he stooped down and wrote on the ground.

9At this, those who heard began to go away one at a time, the older ones first, until only Jesus was left, with the woman still standing there. 10Jesus straightened up and asked her, 'Woman, where are they? Has no-one condemned you?'
11'No-one, sir,' she said.
'Then neither do I condemn you,' Jesus declared. 'Go now and leave your life of sin.'

This passage is no longer regarded as being part of the original Gospel of John and does not appear in modern translations. It does not appear in the best early Greek manuscripts. It is sometimes located here, within brackets, or at the end of the Gospel. The story has more in common with those told in the other Gospels and is best understood as a piece of floating tradition, an example of 'the other things that Jesus did' (21.25) that the author refers to at the very end of this Gospel.

23

The Plot Thickens: Light in the Darkness

John 8.12–59

12When Jesus spoke again to the people, he said, 'I am the light of the world. Whoever follows me will never walk in darkness, but will have the light of life.'

13The Pharisees challenged him, 'Here you are, appearing as your own witness; your testimony is not valid.'

14Jesus answered, 'Even if I testify on my own behalf, my testimony is valid, for I know where I came from and where I am going. But you have no idea where I come from or where I am going. 15You judge by human standards; I pass judgment on no-one. 16But if I do judge, my decisions are right, because I am not alone. I stand with the Father, who sent me. 17In your own Law it is written that the testimony of two men is valid. 18I am one who testifies for myself; my other witness is the Father, who sent me.'

19Then they asked him, 'Where is your father?'

'You do not know me or my Father,' Jesus replied. 'If you knew me, you would know my Father also.' 20He spoke these words while teaching in the temple area near the place where the offerings were put. Yet no-one seized him, because his time had not yet come.

21Once more Jesus said to them, 'I am going away, and you will look for me, and you will die in your sin. Where I go, you cannot come.'

22This made the Jews ask, 'Will he kill himself? Is that why he says, "Where I go, you cannot come"?'

23But he continued, 'You are from below; I am from above. You are of this world; I am not of this world. 24I told you that you would die in your sins; if you do not believe that I am [the one I claim to be], you will indeed die in your sins.'

25'Who are you?' they asked.

'Just what I have been claiming all along,' Jesus replied. 26'I have much to say in judgment of you. But he who sent me is reliable, and what I have heard from him I tell the world.'

27They did not understand that he was telling them about his Father. 28So Jesus said, 'When you have lifted up the Son of Man, then you will know that I am [the one I claim to be] and that I do nothing on my own but speak just what the Father has taught me. 29The one who sent me is with me; he has not left me alone, for I always do what pleases him.' 30Even as he spoke, many put their faith in him.

31To the Jews who had believed him, Jesus said, 'If you hold to my teaching, you are really my disciples. 32Then you will know the truth, and the truth will set you free.'

33They answered him, 'We are Abraham's

descendants and have never been slaves of anyone. How can you say that we shall be set free?'

³⁴Jesus replied, 'I tell you the truth, everyone who sins is a slave to sin. ³⁵Now a slave has no permanent place in the family, but a son belongs to it for ever. ³⁶So if the Son sets you free, you will be free indeed. ³⁷I know you are Abraham's descendants. Yet you are ready to kill me, because you have no room for my word. ³⁸I am telling you what I have seen in the Father's presence, and you do what you have heard from your father.'

³⁹'Abraham is our father,' they answered.

'If you were Abraham's children,' said Jesus, 'then you would do the things Abraham did. ⁴⁰As it is, you are determined to kill me, a man who has told you the truth that I heard from God. Abraham did not do such things. ⁴¹You are doing the things your own father does.'

'We are not illegitimate children,' they protested. 'The only Father we have is God himself.'

⁴²Jesus said to them, 'If God were your Father, you would love me, for I came from God and now am here. I have not come on my own; but he sent me. ⁴³Why is my language not clear to you? Because you are unable to hear what I say. ⁴⁴You belong to your father, the devil, and you want to carry out your father's desire. He was a murderer from the beginning, not holding to the truth, for there is no truth in him. When he lies, he speaks his native language, for he is a liar and the father of lies. ⁴⁵Yet because I tell the truth, you do

not believe me! ⁴⁶Can any of you prove me guilty of sin? If I am telling the truth, why don't you believe me? ⁴⁷He who belongs to God hears what God says. The reason you do not hear is that you do not belong to God.'

⁴⁸The Jews answered him, 'Aren't we right in saying that you are a Samaritan and demon-possessed?'

⁴⁹'I am not possessed by a demon,' said Jesus, 'but I honour my Father and you dishonour me. ⁵⁰I am not seeking glory for myself; but there is one who seeks it, and he is the judge. ⁵¹I tell you the truth, if anyone keeps my word, he will never see death.'

⁵²At this the Jews exclaimed, 'Now we know that you are demon-possessed! Abraham died and so did the prophets, yet you say that if anyone keeps your word, he will never taste death. ⁵³Are you greater than our father Abraham? He died, and so did the prophets. Who do you think you are?'

⁵⁴Jesus replied, 'If I glorify myself, my glory means nothing. My Father, whom you claim as your God, is the one who glorifies me. ⁵⁵Though you do not know him, I know him. If I said I did not, I would be a liar like you, but I do know him and keep his word. ⁵⁶Your father Abraham rejoiced at the thought of seeing my day; he saw it and was glad.'

⁵⁷'You are not yet fifty years old,' the Jews said to him, 'and you have seen Abraham!'

⁵⁸'I tell you the truth,' Jesus answered, 'before Abraham was born, I am!' ⁵⁹At this, they picked up stones to stone him, but Jesus hid himself, slipping away from the temple grounds.

This chapter offers a kind of sub-plot to the main drama of the Gospel as a whole. For the evangelist it is important to stress that he sees Jesus as the one whom the Father has sent into the world to redeem the world, as a light into the darkness of opposition and unbelief. In this chapter the focus is on the opponents of Jesus and what motivates them into opposition. As the Father has sent Jesus as light, this chapter will attempt to show the devil has sent his children the 'Jews' to destroy the light that Jesus represents.

The setting is the same as the previous chapter. We are still in the temple precincts during the feast of Tabernacles when the four golden candlesticks were lit in the Court of the Women. At this point Jesus declares himself to be 'the light of the world' (v. 12). The temple light was said to illuminate every courtyard in Jerusalem. Now that Jesus claims to light up not just the city but the whole world, he becomes the subject of contention. Although the light is not mentioned again, those who have read the prologue will know that the light exists as a source of illumination and witness. In the rest of the chapter it is the origin and veracity of this witness which is under dispute by those whose intention is to destroy him.

There can be no doubt that the tone of this chapter is confrontational. Such an attack on the Pharisees is not confined to this Gospel. Matthew 23 has Jesus making another great denunciation of Pharisaic hypocrisy. In this instance, the attack is far more serious. Jesus is denouncing the 'Jews' for their opposition to his mission and their apparent perversity in misrepresenting him as a 'Samaritan' and 'demon-possessed' (v. 48). In his turn Jesus accuses his opponents of being children of the devil, the 'father of lies and a murderer' (v. 44). In contrast to this Jesus claims to be speaking the truth which his opponents choose not to hear.

At first glance this may all seem a bit puerile, rather like the kind of name-calling which children indulge in at playtime or in the street. Our reaction might be to think that if this is a reflection of the sort of debate going on between Jews and Christians then maybe they could have done better. However, we do have to remember that in the ancient world this sort of rhetoric was common. When someone was called upon to defend themselves from attack they would often respond in like manner. The subject is a volatile and a controversial one concerning the paternity of Jesus or, more importantly, where he comes from. He establishes his credibility (and by token that of his followers) by stressing his dependence on God. His likeness to God is attested by his employing the 'I am' formula usually associated with the divine name (v. 58). What began as a trial of Jesus' paternity ends thus, with Jesus sitting in judgement on his opponents. They so dislike what they hear that they try to stone Jesus (v. 59), but once again the elusive Jesus gives them the slip.

- The pattern of misunderstanding in this chapter is one most of us have experienced at some time or other. The reliance on set forms of rhetorical argument may be foreign, but we all know how important it is to win an argument. Do you think that Jesus was merely concerned to win the argument or was there another motive?

- How should we talk to those of differing faiths? We normally adopt a more polite posture than that displayed in this chapter. Can a more confrontational stance sometimes be justified?

- Would you classify this debate as an interfaith discussion or more of a family row?

- What does Jesus mean when he says, 'If anyone keeps my word, he will never see death' (v. 51)?

24

A Blind Man has Real Insight

John 9.1–41

¹**As he went along, he saw a man blind** from birth. ²His disciples asked him, 'Rabbi, who sinned, this man or his parents, that he was born blind?'

³'Neither this man nor his parents sinned,' said Jesus, 'but this happened so that the work of God might be displayed in his life. ⁴As long as it is day, we must do the work of him who sent me. Night is coming, when no-one can work. ⁵While I am in the world, I am the light of the world.'

⁶Having said this, he spat on the ground, made some mud with the saliva, and put it on the man's eyes. ⁷'Go,' he told him, 'wash in the Pool of Siloam' (this word means Sent). So the man went and washed, and came home seeing. ⁸His neighbours and those who had formerly seen him begging asked, 'Isn't this the same man who used to sit and beg?' ⁹Some claimed that he was.

Others said, 'No, he only looks like him.'

But he himself insisted, 'I am the man.'

¹⁰'How then were your eyes opened?' they demanded.

¹¹He replied, 'The man they call Jesus made some mud and put it on my eyes. He told me to go to Siloam and wash. So I went and washed, and then I could see.'

¹²'Where is this man?' they asked him.

'I don't know,' he said.

¹³They brought to the Pharisees the man who had been blind. ¹⁴Now the day on which Jesus had made the mud and opened the man's eyes was a Sabbath. ¹⁵Therefore the Pharisees also asked him how he had received his sight. 'He put mud on my eyes,' the man replied, 'and I washed, and now I see.'

¹⁶Some of the Pharisees said, 'This man is not from God, for he does not keep the Sabbath.' But others asked, 'How can a sinner do such miraculous signs?' So they were divided.

¹⁷Finally they turned again to the blind man, 'What have you to say about him? It was your eyes he opened.'

The man replied, 'He is a prophet.'

¹⁸The Jews still did not believe that he had been blind and had received his sight until they sent for the man's parents. ¹⁹'Is this your son?' they asked. 'Is this the one you say was born blind? How is it that now he can see?'

²⁰'We know he is our son,' the parents answered, 'and we know he was born blind. ²¹But how he can see now, or who opened his eyes, we don't know. Ask him. He is of age; he will speak for himself.' ²²His parents said this because they were afraid of the Jews, for already the Jews had decided that anyone who acknowledged that Jesus was the Christ would be put out of the synagogue. ²³That was why his parents said, 'He is of age; ask him.'

[24]A second time they summoned the man who had been blind. 'Give glory to God,' they said. 'We know this man is a sinner.' [25]He replied, 'Whether he is a sinner or not, I don't know. One thing I do know. I was blind but now I see!' [26]Then they asked him, 'What did he do to you? How did he open your eyes?' [27]He answered, 'I have told you already and you did not listen. Why do you want to hear it again? Do you want to become his disciples, too?' [28]Then they hurled insults at him and said, 'You are this fellow's disciple! We are disciples of Moses! [29]We know that God spoke to Moses, but as for this fellow, we don't even know where he comes from.' [30]The man answered, 'Now that is remarkable! You don't know where he comes from, yet he opened my eyes. [31]We know that God does not listen to sinners. He listens to the godly man who does his will. [32]Nobody has ever heard of opening the eyes of a man born blind. [33]If this man were not from God, he could do nothing.'

[34]To this they replied, 'You were steeped in sin at birth; how dare you lecture us!' And they threw him out. [35]Jesus heard that they had thrown him out, and when he found him, he said, 'Do you believe in the Son of Man?' [36]'Who is he, sir?' the man asked. 'Tell me so that I may believe in him.' [37]Jesus said, 'You have now seen him; in fact, he is the one speaking with you.' [38]Then the man said, 'Lord, I believe,' and he worshipped him. [39]Jesus said, 'For judgment I have come into this world, so that the blind will see and those who see will become blind.' [40]Some Pharisees who were with him heard him say this and asked, 'What? Are we blind too?' [41]Jesus said, 'If you were blind, you would not be guilty of sin; but now that you claim you can see, your guilt remains.

This chapter contains some of the funniest dialogue in the Bible and yet it has a very serious message; one that a blind man can recognize. As with the story of blind Bartimaeus in the other Gospels (Mark 10.46–52 and parallels), the blind see more clearly than the sighted.

As with the previous two chapters, we are still at the feast of Tabernacles when there is a stress on the twin themes of water and light. Both these themes reappear in this story of the man born blind, who first sees the light in the literal sense on his return from the Pool of Siloam. Jesus had sent him there after making a paste with spit with which he anointed the man's eyes. In chapter 8 we saw Jesus proclaim himself as the 'light of the world'; now we see this illumination at work at both a physical and a spiritual level. The disciples see the blind man and are more interested in doctrinal questions about who is responsible for his plight than his need to see. They are blind to the possibility that God might work a sign through this man. A sign that will illuminate the question of who Jesus is.

The story becomes amusing when the bewildered man is hauled up before the Pharisees. As usual in this Gospel they are diverted, this time by the issue of a Sabbath day healing. To some of them this is proof enough that Jesus is a sinner and cannot come from God, but others see the healing as a sign (v. 16). As there is a division among them they ask the blind man what he thinks. By this time he has reached the conclusion that Jesus is a prophet (v. 17). The 'Jews' do not like the sound of that and begin to cast doubts on the authenticity of the healing. The parents are summoned, but they clearly do not want to get involved, and tell the Jewish hierarchy to apply their interrogation to their son, who is of age. The evangelist tells us that they are fearful of the 'Jews'. What we have in this story is the kind of situation that many of John's first readers were experiencing, as those who confessed Jesus to be the Christ were expelled from the synagogue. The healed man is recalled for further questioning but, unlike the paralytic in the story in chapter 5, which closely echoes this story, the man is not intimidated by his accusers, who charge him with providing false testimony. The man develops in stature, first in confessing he had known nothing of Jesus but now knew him to be a prophet. Then by verse 33 he concludes that Jesus is from God. Five verses later the final confession is that Jesus is 'Lord'.

What is beguiling about this character is his stubborn refusal to be intimidated by the bullying authorities. His cocky answers so upset the interrogators that they throw him out of the synagogue. Many of John's readers would have found immense comfort in these verses about the plucky hero. His expulsion was not a disaster, for he finds himself in the presence of Jesus, whom he is able to worship. This once-blind man 'sees' Jesus as he really is. Some of the Pharisees see the implications for themselves in all this (v. 40). They are presented as the real sinners, for in John a sinner is one who will not believe. In contrast to this the blind man is seen as a model disciple who displays many of the characteristics we have seen in Jesus himself. Like the good disciple he imitates his master.

- Does the man born blind provide a model for true discipleship in John's Gospel?

- Where is there spiritual blindness today? How is it characterized?

- Can you think of a situation when a religious group might enforce an excommunication order?

- Do you think the reply of Jesus (v. 3) is a satisfactory explanation for physical or mental impairment from birth? If not, how do you account for it?

25

The Shepherd as a Doormat

John 10.1–42

¹'I tell you the truth, the man who does not enter the sheep pen by the gate, but climbs in by some other way, is a thief and a robber. ²The man who enters by the gate is the shepherd of his sheep. ³The watchman opens the gate for him, and the sheep listen to his voice. He calls his own sheep by name and leads them out. ⁴When he has brought out all his own, he goes on ahead of them, and his sheep follow him because they know his voice. ⁵But they will never follow a stranger; in fact, they will run away from him because they do not recognise a stranger's voice.' ⁶Jesus used this figure of speech, but they did not understand what he was telling them.

⁷Therefore Jesus said again, 'I tell you the truth, I am the gate for the sheep. ⁸All who ever came before me were thieves and robbers, but the sheep did not listen to them. ⁹I am the gate; whoever enters through me will be saved. He will come in and go out, and find pasture. ¹⁰The thief comes only to steal and kill and destroy; I have come that they may have life, and have it to the full.

¹¹'I am the good shepherd. The good shepherd lays down his life for the sheep. ¹²The hired hand is not the shepherd who owns the sheep. So when he sees the wolf coming, he abandons the sheep and runs away. Then the wolf attacks the flock and scatters it. ¹³The man runs away because he is a hired hand and cares nothing for the sheep.

¹⁴'I am the good shepherd; I know my sheep and my sheep know me—¹⁵just as the Father knows me and I know the Father—and I lay down my life for the sheep. ¹⁶I have other sheep that are not of this sheep pen. I must bring them also. They too will listen to my voice, and there shall be one flock and one shepherd. ¹⁷The reason my Father loves me is that I lay down my life—only to take it up again. ¹⁸No-one takes it from me, but I lay it down of my own accord. I have authority to lay it down and authority to take it up again. This command I received from my Father.'

¹⁹At these words the Jews were again divided. ²⁰Many of them said, 'He is demon-possessed and raving mad. Why listen to him?' ²¹But others said, 'These are not the sayings of a man possessed by a demon. Can a demon open the eyes of the blind?'

²²Then came the Feast of Dedication at Jerusalem. It was winter, ²³and Jesus was in the temple area walking in Solomon's Colonnade. ²⁴The Jews gathered round him, saying, 'How long will you keep us in suspense? If you are the Christ, tell us plainly.' ²⁵Jesus answered, 'I did tell you, but you do

not believe. The miracles I do in my Father's name speak for me, ²⁶but you do not believe because you are not my sheep. ²⁷My sheep listen to my voice; I know them, and they follow me. ²⁸I give them eternal life, and they shall never perish; no-one can snatch them out of my hand. ²⁹My Father, who has given them to me, is greater than all; no-one can snatch them out of my Father's hand. ³⁰I and the Father are one.'

³¹Again the Jews picked up stones to stone him, ³²but Jesus said to them, 'I have shown you many great miracles from the Father. For which of these do you stone me?'

³³'We are not stoning you for any of these,' replied the Jews, 'but for blasphemy, because you, a mere man, claim to be God.'

³⁴Jesus answered them, 'Is it not written in your Law, "I have said you are gods"? ³⁵If he called them "gods", to whom the word of God came—and the Scripture cannot be broken—³⁶what about the one whom the Father set apart as his very own and sent into the world? Why then do you accuse me of blasphemy because I said, "I am God's Son"? ³⁷Do not believe me unless I do what my Father does. ³⁸But if I do it, even though you do not believe me, believe the miracles, that you may know and understand that the Father is in me, and I in the Father.' ³⁹Again they tried to seize him, but he escaped their grasp.

⁴⁰Then Jesus went back across the Jordan to the place where John had been baptising in the early days. Here he stayed ⁴¹and many people came to him. They said, 'Though John never performed a miraculous sign, all that John said about this man was true.' ⁴²And in that place many believed in Jesus.

The pastoral role of Jesus is very important in this Gospel, written for those who find themselves ejected from their religious base in the synagogue. The man born blind, who appeared in the previous chapter, was ejected for his confession of faith in Jesus. So Jesus, as the good pastor, sought him out and welcomed him to the new fold of those who hear and respond to his voice. In this chapter John draws out the implications of the new pastoral community who have inherited the role of the people of God.

Unlike the other Gospels, John does not contain parables. The preferred mode is that of long discussions whereby Jesus instructs his disciples and they ask the odd question. In the first six verses of this chapter we get very near to a parable in what John calls a 'figure of speech'. This term means a symbolic word-picture with a hidden meaning. Sadly, the disciples did not understand the 'figure' (v. 6), and Jesus has to interpret the meaning for them. We too may have difficulties in 'reading' this figure of the shepherd. We no longer live in a pastoral society where sheep are guarded by the life of the shepherd, who literally lays his body down at the entrance of a sheepfold in order to protect the life of his flock. Our idea of a 'good shepherd' probably has more to do with Marie Antoinette and stained glass than Middle-Eastern hill farmers warding off predators night after night in the lambing season.

Once the disciples have the figure explained they can see clearly that the pastoral role of Jesus in caring for his flock involves much more than was on offer by the nation's previous shepherds, who by their dereliction of duty no longer deserve that title and are now described as 'thieves and robbers' (v. 8). Their legacy is one of theft and destruction of their sacred charge (v. 8). Ezekiel in chapter 34 makes a similar attack on the leaders of Israel who have forfeited their right to be called shepherds. In this chapter Jesus repeatedly promises to lay down his life for the sheep (vv. 11, 15, 17, 18), and he does this of his own accord in response to his sacred charge (v. 18). The reason for this sacrificial offer is that his new flock might have 'life in all its fullness' (v. 10). The good shepherd is the physical gateway to new and eternal life. By his self-offering they are protected from molestation and death (v. 28). The fact that all this takes place at the feast of Dedication (v. 22) is John's way of saying that the dedication of Jesus to his flock far exceeds that offered by the temple and its ritual, which he has come to replace (2.13–22).

Such language is too much for the 'Jews', and there is division among them as to what motivates him. Is he demonized or does he speak for God? As in the other Gospels, when the Baptist is concerned to know who Jesus is, Jesus points to the works he is doing and asks his questioners to believe the evidence of their eyes (vv. 37–8). If they are open to the workings of God in him then they will see that the Father is in him and he is the Son of God. As if to reinforce this, Jesus uses the 'I am' formula several times in this chapter. Again their attempts to arrest or stone him are foiled, and Jesus retires to a place of safety where many come and believe in him there (v. 42).

• Is the image of Jesus as the 'good shepherd' helpful or not?

• Can you think of a more relevant image for our society today?

- What does the picture of a shepherd whose voice is known by the sheep say to our society today?

- Can we recover a sense of pastoral care which reflects the relationship that the Son has with the Father? If so how might it be achieved?

26

The Final Sign: A Tomb Is Opened

John 11.1–54

¹**Now a man named Lazarus was sick. He** was from Bethany, the village of Mary and her sister Martha. ²This Mary, whose brother Lazarus now lay sick, was the same one who poured perfume on the Lord and wiped his feet with her hair. ³So the sisters sent word to Jesus, 'Lord, the one you love is sick.' ⁴When he heard this, Jesus said, 'This sickness will not end in death. No, it is for God's glory so that God's Son may be glorified through it.' ⁵Jesus loved Martha and her sister and Lazarus. ⁶Yet when he heard that Lazarus was sick, he stayed where he was two more days. ⁷Then he said to his disciples, 'Let us go back to Judea.'

⁸'But Rabbi,' they said, 'a short while ago the Jews tried to stone you, and yet you are going back there?'

⁹Jesus answered, 'Are there not twelve hours of daylight? A man who walks by day will not stumble, for he sees by this world's light. ¹⁰It is when he walks by night that he stumbles, for he has no light.'

¹¹After he had said this, he went on to tell them, 'Our friend Lazarus has fallen asleep; but I am going there to wake him up.'

¹²His disciples replied, 'Lord, if he sleeps, he will get better.' ¹³Jesus had been speaking of his death, but his disciples thought he meant natural sleep.

¹⁴So then he told them plainly, 'Lazarus is dead, ¹⁵and for your sake I am glad I was not there, so that you may believe. But let us go to him.'

¹⁶Then Thomas (called Didymus) said to the rest of the disciples, 'Let us also go, that we may die with him.'

¹⁷On his arrival, Jesus found that Lazarus had already been in the tomb for four days. ¹⁸Bethany was less than two miles from Jerusalem, ¹⁹and many Jews had come to Martha and Mary to comfort them in the loss of their brother. ²⁰When Martha heard that Jesus was coming, she went out to meet him, but Mary stayed at home.

²¹'Lord,' Martha said to Jesus, 'if you had been here, my brother would not have died. ²²But I know that even now God will give you whatever you ask.'

²³Jesus said to her, 'Your brother will rise again.'

²⁴Martha answered, 'I know he will rise again in the resurrection at the last day.'

²⁵Jesus said to her, 'I am the resurrection and the life. He who believes in me will live, even though he dies; ²⁶and whoever lives and believes in me will never die. Do you believe this?'

²⁷'Yes, Lord,' she told him, 'I believe that you are the Christ, the Son of God, who was to

come into the world.'

²⁸And after she had said this, she went back and called her sister Mary aside. 'The Teacher is here,' she said, 'and is asking for you.' ²⁹When Mary heard this, she got up quickly and went to him. ³⁰Now Jesus had not yet entered the village, but was still at the place where Martha had met him. ³¹When the Jews who had been with Mary in the house, comforting her, noticed how quickly she got up and went out, they followed her, supposing she was going to the tomb to mourn there.

³²When Mary reached the place where Jesus was and saw him, she fell at his feet and said, 'Lord, if you had been here, my brother would not have died.'

³³When Jesus saw her weeping, and the Jews who had come along with her also weeping, he was deeply moved in spirit and troubled. ³⁴'Where have you laid him?' he asked.

'Come and see, Lord,' they replied.

³⁵Jesus wept.

³⁶Then the Jews said, 'See how he loved him!' ³⁷But some of them said, 'Could not he who opened the eyes of the blind man have kept this man from dying?'

³⁸Jesus, once more deeply moved, came to the tomb. It was a cave with a stone laid across the entrance. ³⁹'Take away the stone,' he said.

'But, Lord,' said Martha, the sister of the dead man, 'by this time there is a bad odour, for he has been there four days.'

⁴⁰Then Jesus said, 'Did I not tell you that if you believed, you would see the glory of God?'

⁴¹So they took away the stone. Then Jesus looked up and said, 'Father, I thank you that you have heard me. ⁴²I knew that you always hear me, but I said this for the benefit of the people standing here, that they may believe that you sent me.'

⁴³When he had said this, Jesus called in a loud voice, 'Lazarus, come out!' ⁴⁴The dead man came out, his hands and feet wrapped with strips of linen, and a cloth around his face.

Jesus said to them, 'Take off the grave clothes and let him go.'

⁴⁵Therefore many of the Jews who had come to visit Mary, and had seen what Jesus did, put their faith in him. ⁴⁶But some of them went to the Pharisees and told them what Jesus had done. ⁴⁷Then the chief priests and the Pharisees called a meeting of the Sanhedrin.

'What are we accomplishing?' they asked. 'Here is this man performing many miraculous signs. ⁴⁸If we let him go on like this, everyone will believe in him, and then the Romans will come and take away both our place and our nation.'

⁴⁹Then one of them, named Caiaphas, who was high priest that year, spoke up, 'You know nothing at all! ⁵⁰You do not realise that it is better for you that one man die for the people than that the whole nation perish.'

⁵¹He did not say this on his own, but as high priest that year he prophesied that Jesus would die for the Jewish nation, ⁵²and not only for that nation but also for the scattered children of God, to bring them together and make them one. ⁵³So from that day on they plotted to take his life.

⁵⁴Therefore Jesus no longer moved about publicly among the Jews. Instead he withdrew to a region near the desert, to a village called Ephraim, where he stayed with his disciples.

This is a crucial chapter in John's Gospel. This final sign will complete all that has gone before and point to the meaning of the resurrection itself. This miracle will prove to be the deciding factor in the resolve to have Jesus put to death. In giving life to others he himself loses his life. The story begins in the place where Jesus was first to set out on his mission. He has retreated here to avoid the dangers of Jerusalem, where several attempts on his life have been made. No sooner has he arrived than a summons comes from the sisters of his friend Lazarus. Mary and Martha want him to attend to their brother, who is ill. Unaccountably, Jesus deliberately delays his return for two days. The disciples are aware of the danger in returning to the environs of Jerusalem, and do not encourage Jesus to take risks. But when he tells them plainly that Lazarus is dead, only Thomas is perceptive enough to want to return, knowing what is involved and willing to take the consequences (v. 16).

The scene is now set for the sign to be enacted. The disciples and we both know that Lazarus is dead, for we are told this plainly (v. 14). As if to emphasize the point, when Jesus orders the stone to be removed from the tomb Martha complains that there will be a smell. There can be no doubt that Lazarus is dead. The doubt is to do with the idea of 'resurrection'. Martha protests her belief 'in the resurrection at the last day' (v. 24). Jesus corrects her by claiming that he now is 'the resurrection and the life' (v. 25). Martha accepts this and goes on to make a strong confession of faith (v. 27). The issue is, can she sustain this faith? The resuscitation of her brother strains her credulity and that of her sister, who both believed that Jesus could have prevented Lazarus's death but are not so sure about his ability to revive him. In calling Lazarus forth (v. 43), Jesus demonstrates not only his love for this grief-stricken family but also his conviction that God would reveal his glory in this miracle (v. 40). He shouts for life at the tomb, in contrast to the shouts for his death which will occur on Good Friday (18.40; 19.6, 15). John is aware of the paradox in which this offer of life by Jesus will result in his death (v. 50).

The account of the special Council to decide what to do about the growing popularity of Jesus is heavy with irony. The Council recognize that Jesus is performing many signs, but fail to acknowledge their meaning. Indeed their fear is that 'everyone will believe in him' (v. 48) and then the temple will become obsolete or, even worse, the Romans might remove it and the nation. The irony continues in the next few verses: 'It is expedient that one man die for the people' foretells Caiaphas unwittingly (v. 50). The death of Jesus will render all the cultic paraphernalia redundant, including the system that they are so keen to defend and which they mistakenly identify as the soul of their nation. What is the purpose of John telling this story of the raising of Lazarus, which is only to be found in this Gospel? As with everything that John writes, the purpose is to foster faith in Jesus 'as the Christ the Son of God and that in believing we might have life in his name' (20.31). In selecting this story about the revival of a well-loved friend, the writer demonstrates the effect of such a belief. The story is meant to be read and reread. Initially it will not make complete sense as there are a number of references to events that, as yet, have not taken place (e.g. v. 2 refers to Mary's anointing, which happens in the next chapter). As with so much of this Gospel, the reader is meant to make connections forward and back before the picture becomes completely clear. The fact that Lazarus is raised is living proof that life is available to all those who hear and respond to 'the voice of the Son of God' (5.25). John is not concerned to relate a miracle but rather a sign for the spiritually discerning. In this story, so beautifully told, both Mary and Martha come to faith in Jesus. The assurance and the glory of God is seen when their dead brother responds to the voice of Jesus. The significance of the sign is that there is nothing beyond God's saving power, 'he who believes in me even though he die, yet shall he live' says Jesus (v. 25). The beauty of John's theology is that it can be expressed in a convincing story, full of exquisite detail, and this enhances its meaning.

- What connections can you detect in this story with the resurrection of Jesus?

- Is it important to believe that this event actually happened as described or is it better to discern the message behind the story and what it is meant to signify?

- How does the resurrection story in John compare with this section about the raising of Lazarus?

- Do you think the Pharisees had a point regarding the Romans being provoked to 'come and take away both our temple and our nation' (v. 48)?

PLAIN SPEAKING

27

Jesus is Sought Out

John 11.55—12.36

⁵⁵**When it was almost time for the Jewish** Passover, many went up from the country to Jerusalem for their ceremonial cleansing before the Passover. ⁵⁶They kept looking for Jesus, and as they stood in the temple area they asked one another, 'What do you think? Isn't he coming to the Feast at all?' ⁵⁷But the chief priests and Pharisees had given orders that if anyone found out where Jesus was, he should report it so that they might arrest him. ¹²·¹Six days before the Passover, Jesus arrived at Bethany, where Lazarus lived, whom Jesus had raised from the dead. ²Here a dinner was given in Jesus' honour. Martha served, while Lazarus was among those reclining at the table with him. ³Then Mary took about a pint of pure nard, an expensive perfume; she poured it on Jesus' feet and wiped his feet with her hair. And the house was filled with the fragrance of the perfume.

⁴But one of his disciples, Judas Iscariot, who was later to betray him, objected, ⁵'Why wasn't this perfume sold and the money given to the poor? It was worth a year's wages.' ⁶He did not say this because he cared about the poor but because he was a thief; as keeper of the money bag, he used to help himself to what was put into it.

⁷'Leave her alone,' Jesus replied. '[It was intended] that she should save this perfume for the day of my burial. ⁸You will always have the poor among you, but you will not always have me.'

⁹Meanwhile a large crowd of Jews found out that Jesus was there and came, not only because of him but also to see Lazarus, whom he had raised from the dead. ¹⁰So the chief priests made plans to kill Lazarus as well, ¹¹for on account of him many of the Jews were going over to Jesus and putting their faith in him.

¹²The next day the great crowd that had come for the Feast heard that Jesus was on his way to Jerusalem. ¹³They took palm branches and went out to meet him, shouting,

'Hosanna!'

'Blessed is he who comes in the name of the Lord!'

'Blessed is the King of Israel!' [14]Jesus found a young donkey and sat upon it, as it is written, [15]'Do not be afraid, O Daughter of Zion; see, your king is coming, seated on a donkey's colt.' [16]At first his disciples did not understand all this. Only after Jesus was glorified did they realise that these things had been written about him and that they had done these things to him. [17]Now the crowd that was with him when he called Lazarus from the tomb and raised him from the dead continued to spread the word. [18]Many people, because they had heard that he had given this miraculous sign, went out to meet him. [19]So the Pharisees said to one another, 'See, this is getting us nowhere. Look how the whole world has gone after him!'

[20]Now there were some Greeks among those who went up to worship at the Feast. [21]They came to Philip, who was from Bethsaida in Galilee, with a request. 'Sir,' they said, 'we would like to see Jesus.' [22]Philip went to tell Andrew; Andrew and Philip in turn told Jesus. [23]Jesus replied, 'The hour has come for the Son of Man to be glorified. [24]I tell you the truth, unless a grain of wheat falls to the ground and dies, it remains only a single seed. But if it dies, it produces many seeds. [25]The man who loves his life will lose it, while the man who hates his life in this world will keep it for eternal life. [26]Whoever serves me must follow me; and where I am, my servant also will be. My Father will honour the one who serves me.

[27]'Now my heart is troubled, and what shall I say? "Father, save me from this hour"? No, it was for this very reason I came to this hour. [28]Father, glorify your name!'

Then a voice came from heaven, 'I have glorified it, and will glorify it again.' [29]The crowd that was there and heard it said it had thundered; others said an angel had spoken to him.

[30]Jesus said, 'This voice was for your benefit, not mine. [31]Now is the time for judgment on this world; now the prince of this world will be driven out. [32]But I, when I am lifted up from the earth, will draw all men to myself.' [33]He said this to show the kind of death he was going to die.

[34]The crowd spoke up, 'We have heard from the Law that the Christ will remain for ever, so how can you say, "The Son of Man must be lifted up"? Who is this "Son of Man"?'

[35]Then Jesus told them, 'You are going to have the light just a little while longer. Walk while you have the light, before darkness overtakes you. The man who walks in the dark does not know where he is going. [36]Put your trust in the light while you have it, so that you may become sons of light.' When he had finished speaking, Jesus left and hid himself from them.

The clouds darken for Jesus. The final Passover is at hand. Jesus is soon to accomplish his mission of liberating his people from blindness and sin. As at the first Passover, there is an organized opposition. This time the obstruction comes not from Pharaoh, but from the leaders of the Jewish nation, who issue a warrant for the arrest of Jesus (v. 57). As in the Exodus narrative (Exodus 7.3), their hearts are hardened, despite the many signs and wonders which are performed. They will not believe that God is at work in the actions of Jesus. Meanwhile speculation is rife as to whether or not Jesus will show himself at the feast.

Before the final work of salvation is achieved, a number of prophetic signs are set in motion. The first takes place in the home of Lazarus, Mary and Martha. These three are portrayed as exemplary disciples. As in the other Gospels, Martha serves, but this time without complaint. Her sister sits at the feet of Jesus but in an active rather than a passive mode. She breaks open a box of costly ointment and proceeds to anoint Jesus in preparation for his burial. Again, it is the women in this narrative who behave in an exemplary way. By contrast Judas is criticized for being mean-minded (v. 7). This incident should be interpreted as an enacted prophetic sign which points to the coming death of Jesus. Only Mary is able to discern this meaning; Jesus is forced to explain the significance to the other disciples.

Other signs come in quick succession. The reaction to them is mixed. The crowd that arrives at Bethany (v. 9) does so, not in response to the idea that Jesus is bringing new life to the world, but to peep at the newly revived Lazarus. They, like the crowd in chapter 6, are drawn for sensation-seeking reasons rather than prompted by spiritual discernment. The next sign also involves a crowd, this time with a little more insight. They recognize the messianic nature of Jesus' entry into Jerusalem and proclaim him 'king of Israel' (v. 13). John makes this much more clear than the other Gospels, even quoting Zechariah 9.9 in support of his interpretation of this event. Surprisingly, the only people not aware of the significance of this enacted prophetic sign are the disciples, who will not put two and two together until after the resurrection. The Pharisees are at a complete loss. In another touch of Johannine irony they declare that 'the world has gone after him' (v. 19).

An example of this growing global popularity occurs in the next passage when some Greeks appear and enquire of Philip if they might 'see Jesus'. We have already seen how important the theme of seeking Jesus is in this Gospel. The fact that gentiles are now engaged in this religious quest initiates a new development in the story, and Jesus responds by declaring that his long-awaited 'hour' has at last come (v. 23). The coming of the Greeks is the signal that in order for Jesus to achieve his purposes of making God known he, like a grain of wheat, must fall to the ground and die (v. 24). This is the only way his work can bear fruit. Indeed this is the only course of action for any who would follow him. The passage is very reminiscent of the passion predictions in the other Gospels, which is another example of John drawing out what is implicit in the tradition. In this case, John's language parallels that used in the other Gospels when they describe Jesus' agony in the garden. In both cases Jesus prays for deliverance from this 'hour' (v. 27 and Mark 14.35), and his human distress is emphasized as he contemplates his fate. However distressed Jesus is, he is able to master his emotions and focuses on the importance of his vocation to face this hour. The passage ends with a voice from heaven verifying what Jesus is doing and Jesus indicating what sort of death he will die (v. 33). In being 'lifted up' on a cross as a public spectacle he will be an obvious sign to those who seek him as a source of salvation. However, the darkness is approaching. The time for decision and discernment is fast disappearing and, as if to emphasize the point, Jesus withdraws from the scene (v. 36).

- **What is a 'prophetic' sign or action?**

- **Do the actions of Jesus speak louder than his words?**

- **John proclaims that the Word became flesh (1.14). Has he produced enough evidence for others to come to this same conviction? Do the signs we have been noting make this clear?**

- **What do you make of the heavenly voice in verse 28? Does it remind you of significant moments in the other Gospels? Is John alluding to these and making his own connections with the baptism and the transfiguration, linking them with the cross? Luke certainly makes a similar link (Luke 9.31).**

28

A New Commandment

John 12.37—13.38

³⁷**Even after Jesus had done all these** miraculous signs in their presence, they still would not believe in him. ³⁸This was to fulfil the word of Isaiah the prophet:
'Lord, who has believed our message and to whom has the arm of the Lord been revealed?' ³⁹For this reason they could not believe, because, as Isaiah says elsewhere:
⁴⁰'He has blinded their eyes and deadened their hearts, so they can neither see with their eyes, nor understand with their hearts, nor turn—and I would heal them.'
⁴¹Isaiah said this because he saw Jesus' glory and spoke about him.
⁴²Yet at the same time many even among the leaders believed in him. But because of the Pharisees they would not confess their faith for fear they would be put out of the synagogue; ⁴³for they loved praise from men more than praise from God.
⁴⁴Then Jesus cried out, 'When a man believes in me, he does not believe in me only, but in the one who sent me. ⁴⁵When he looks at me, he sees the one who sent me. ⁴⁶I have come into the world as a light, so that no-one who believes in me should stay in darkness.
⁴⁷'As for the person who hears my words but does not keep them, I do not judge him. For I did not come to judge the world, but to save it. ⁴⁸There is a judge for the one who rejects me and does not accept my words; that very word which I spoke will condemn him at the last day. ⁴⁹For I did not speak of my own accord, but the Father who sent me commanded me what to say and how to say it. ⁵⁰I know that his command leads to eternal life. So whatever I say is just what the Father has told me to say.'

¹³:¹It was just before the Passover Feast. Jesus knew that the time had come for him to leave this world and go to the Father. Having loved his own who were in the world, he now showed them the full extent of his love.

²The evening meal was being served, and the devil had already prompted Judas Iscariot, son of Simon, to betray Jesus. ³Jesus knew that the Father had put all things under his power, and that he had come from God and was returning to God; ⁴so he got up from the meal, took off his outer clothing, and wrapped a towel round his waist. ⁵After that, he poured water into a basin and began to wash his disciples' feet, drying them with the towel that was wrapped round him.

⁶He came to Simon Peter, who said to him, 'Lord, are you going to wash my feet?' ⁷Jesus replied, 'You do not realise now what I am doing, but later you will understand.'

[8]'No,' said Peter, 'you shall never wash my feet.'

Jesus answered, 'Unless I wash you, you have no part with me.'

[9]'Then, Lord,' Simon Peter replied, 'not just my feet but my hands and my head as well!'

[10]Jesus answered, 'A person who has had a bath needs only to wash his feet; his whole body is clean. And you are clean, though not every one of you.' [11]For he knew who was going to betray him, and that was why he said not every one was clean.

[12]When he had finished washing their feet, he put on his clothes and returned to his place. 'Do you understand what I have done for you?' he asked them. [13]'You call me "Teacher" and "Lord", and rightly so, for that is what I am. [14]Now that I, your Lord and Teacher, have washed your feet, you also should wash one another's feet. [15]I have set you an example that you should do as I have done for you. [16]I tell you the truth, no servant is greater than his master, nor is a messenger greater than the one who sent him. [17]Now that you know these things, you will be blessed if you do them.

[18]'I am not referring to all of you; I know those I have chosen. But this is to fulfil the scripture: "He who shares my bread has lifted up his heel against me."

[19]'I am telling you now before it happens, so that when it does happen you will believe that I am He. [20]I tell you the truth, whoever accepts anyone I send accepts me; and whoever accepts me accepts the one who sent me.'

[21]After he had said this, Jesus was troubled in spirit and testified, 'I tell you the truth, one of you is going to betray me.'

[22]His disciples stared at one another, at a loss to know which of them he meant. [23]One of them, the disciple whom Jesus loved, was reclining next to him. [24]Simon Peter motioned to this disciple and said, 'Ask him which one he means.'

[25]Leaning back against Jesus, he asked him, 'Lord, who is it?'

[26]Jesus answered, 'It is the one to whom I will give this piece of bread when I have dipped it in the dish.' Then, dipping the piece of bread, he gave it to Judas Iscariot, son of Simon. [27]As soon as Judas took the bread, Satan entered into him.

'What you are about to do, do quickly,' Jesus told him, [28]but no-one at the meal understood why Jesus said this to him. [29]Since Judas had charge of the money, some thought Jesus was telling him to buy what was needed for the Feast, or to give something to the poor. [30]As soon as Judas had taken the bread, he went out. And it was night.

[31]When he was gone, Jesus said, 'Now is the Son of Man glorified and God is glorified in him. [32]If God is glorified in him, God will glorify the Son in himself, and will glorify him at once. [33]'My children, I will be with you only a little longer. You will look for me, and just as I told the Jews, so I tell you now: Where I am going, you cannot come.

[34]'A new command I give you: Love one another. As I have loved you, so you must love one another. [35]By this all men will know that you are my disciples, if you love one another.'

[36]Simon Peter asked him, 'Lord, where are you going?'

Jesus replied, 'Where I am going, you cannot follow now, but you will follow later.'

³⁷Peter asked, 'Lord, why can't I follow you now? I will lay down my life for you.' ³⁸Then Jesus answered, 'Will you really lay down your life for me? I tell you the truth, before the cock crows, you will disown me three times!

Before the so-called 'Book of Signs' ends, the narrator concludes with a passage about the futility of their effect among the unbelieving (v. 7). As the Book of Signs began with a reference to Isaiah (1.23), it now closes with another quotation in which blindness and hardness of heart are foretold. The reference adds Isaiah as another Old Testament witness to the significance of Jesus and his message of salvation. Those who fail to see the significance of the signs that Jesus has enacted in their presence have passed judgement on themselves (v. 47). The Book of Signs ends as it began, with allusions to light in the darkness (i.e. 12.46; 1.19), seeing glory (i.e. 12.41; 1.14) and the relation of the Son to the Father. In fact this section is a series of flashbacks dealing with many of the themes covered in the first part of the Gospel. It also points to what is to come in the second half of the Gospel. From now until the passion narrative there is no reference to time or place; Jesus simply 'cries out' (v. 44) a series of significant truths as the door into heaven is pushed open to reveal that Jesus is speaking, not his own words, but those of the Father. These are the words of eternal life (v. 50). The reason why this Gospel was written is that those who read it may experience that life (20.31). For the next five chapters this theme will be developed in what are called 'farewell discourses' in which the reader is privileged to share in the intimate private world which the disciples share with their Master as he reveals to them the words of eternal life.

The next few chapters cover a period of twenty-four hours from the Last Supper to the Day of Preparation. This is a much shorter period than anything else we have encountered so far. From now on the intensity heightens; Jesus has come to his 'hour' (13.1). Apart from the narrative of the 'feet-washing' which takes place at supper, the rest of this section takes the form of long speech interspersed by the odd comment from the awed disciples. The section begins with an enacted parable, that of the feet-washing. This is a farewell gesture by which Jesus reinforces his teaching about the new kind of love which must be the hallmark of the Christian community. By it Jesus provides an example of how his followers should behave, and ensures that his disciples will continue to be part of him and he of them after he is taken from them in a physical sense. The enigmatic nature of this dramatic sign is apparent from the way that the disciples, Peter in particular, are unable to understand what is happening. As is usual in this Gospel, Jesus is in full command; he knows he is returning to God (v. 3), he is aware of who it is who will betray him (v. 21), and he knows Peter will deny him three times (v. 38). Jesus will reveal all this in due course and at the right moment. Meanwhile the feet-washing continues and the disciples must learn its significance.

Three characters emerge in the text: Peter, Judas and the 'beloved disciple'. Peter and Judas are dealt with elsewhere, but the 'beloved disciple' is a character who has a certain importance in this Gospel which is worth exploring. The identity of this disciple is never revealed. Tradition has it that this is the John the son of Zebedee and the brother of James after whom the Gospel is named. Others think 'the disciple whom Jesus loved' refers to Lazarus, who is described in similar terms in chapter 11. In chapter 12 Lazarus is described as reclining with Jesus at supper (12.2). Whoever the beloved disciple is, he is meant to be seen as a model of discipleship and one for whom the writer of this Gospel has special respect. In this passage he shares an intimate relationship with Jesus which gives rise to the term 'bosom friend'. The relationship has a deeper significance in that it is meant to be a reflection of the relationship that Jesus enjoys with the Father (1.18) and is something all believers are expected to experience as beloved chidren of God (1.12).

Finally, it has to be said that the foot-washing episode conveys many of the themes that the breaking of the bread explores in the other Gospels. Essentially both are dramatic or prophetic signs that Jesus is saying goodbye to his disciples and yet leaving them with a legacy which will strengthen their fellowship and reveal something of the nature and purpose of his death. So in this context Jesus is seen to make himself vulnerable, he lays aside his garments as he will do on the cross. Then by the use of water he purifies his disciples into a union with him (v. 8). This 'indwelling' of the disciples and Jesus is sealed in the command to love one another (v. 34). It is in response to the law of love that Jesus is 'lifted up', and elevated in glory.

- Why do you think John's Gospel fails to give us an account of the 'breaking of bread' at the Last Supper? -

- What is the purpose of the story of the foot-washing? Does it have sacramental overtones?

- Why do you think the author of this Gospel prefers to talk of 'the beloved disciple' rather than to give him a name?

29

Jesus Opens the Door to the Father

John 14.1–31

¹'Do not let your hearts be troubled. Trust in God; trust also in me. ²In my Father's house are many rooms; if it were not so, I would have told you. I am going there to prepare a place for you. ³And if I go and prepare a place for you, I will come back and take you to be with me that you also may be where I am. ⁴You know the way to the place where I am going.'

⁵Thomas said to him, 'Lord, we don't know where you are going, so how can we know the way?'

⁶Jesus answered, 'I am the way and the truth and the life. No-one comes to the Father except through me. ⁷If you really knew me, you would know my Father as well. From now on, you do know him and have seen him.'

⁸Philip said, 'Lord, show us the Father and that will be enough for us.'

⁹Jesus answered: 'Don't you know me, Philip, even after I have been among you such a long time? Anyone who has seen me has seen the Father. How can you say, "Show us the Father"? ¹⁰Don't you believe that I am in the Father, and that the Father is in me? The words I say to you are not just my own. Rather, it is the Father, living in me, who is doing his work. ¹¹Believe me when I say that I am in the Father and the Father is in me; or at least believe on the evidence of the miracles themselves. ¹²I tell you the truth, anyone who has faith in me will do what I have been doing. He will do even greater things than these, because I am going to the Father. ¹³And I will do whatever you ask in my name, so that the Son may bring glory to the Father. ¹⁴You may ask me for anything in my name, and I will do it.

¹⁵'If you love me, you will obey what I command. ¹⁶And I will ask the Father, and he will give you another Counsellor to be with you for ever—¹⁷the Spirit of truth. The world cannot accept him, because it neither sees him nor knows him. But you know him, for he lives with you and will be in you. ¹⁸I will not leave you as orphans; I will come to you. ¹⁹Before long, the world will not see me any more, but you will see me. Because I live, you also will live. ²⁰On that day you will realise that I am in my Father, and you are in me, and I am in you. ²¹Whoever has my commands and obeys them, he is the one who loves me. He who loves me will be loved by my Father, and I too will love him and show myself to him.'

²²Then Judas (not Judas Iscariot) said, 'But, Lord, why do you intend to show yourself to us and not to the world?'

²³Jesus replied, 'If anyone loves me, he will

obey my teaching. My Father will love him, and we will come to him and make our home with him. [24]He who does not love me will not obey my teaching. These words you hear are not my own; they belong to the Father who sent me.

[25]'All this I have spoken while still with you. [26]But the Counsellor, the Holy Spirit, whom the Father will send in my name, will teach you all things and will remind you of everything I have said to you. [27]Peace I leave with you; my peace I give you. I do not give to you as the world gives. Do not let your hearts be troubled and do not be afraid. [28]'You heard me say, "I am going away and I am coming back to you." If you loved me, you would be glad that I am going to the Father, for the Father is greater than I. [29]I have told you now before it happens, so that when it does happen you will believe. [30]I will not speak with you much longer, for the prince of this world is coming. He has no hold on me, [31]but the world must learn that I love the Father and that I do exactly what my Father has commanded me. 'Come now; let us leave.

In the great heroic tradition, Jesus makes his 'farewell discourse' to his followers on the eve of his death. In an age which viewed death with more equanimity than we do today, such a literary device was common. Whether or not heroes actually made such grand speeches, their devotees would compose them as a tribute to the great men that they wished to commemorate. The nearest thing we have in our society is the obituary which is presented as a tribute after death. In the case of a farewell discourse the speech comes before the death and is in the form of a solemn commission and exhortation to the followers to continue in the tradition of their leader.

The contemporary Jewish historian, Josephus, composed similar speeches and put one into the mouth of the Zealot champion, Eleazar. The farewell speech is 'delivered' on the eve of a mass suicide on Masada before the Roman capture of that last stronghold of resistance on the shores of the Dead Sea. Here in chapters 13 to 17 of John we have a similar form which has many Old Testament parallels (e.g. the speech of Moses in Deuteronomy 31–33). In both these examples the speaker exhorts his hearers to be strong and courageous in the face of difficulty and overwhelming odds.

Jesus assures the disciples that they are not left alone even though Jesus himself is leaving them to return to the Father. They are being prepared for a situation that John's community are now having to accept and cope with. They will eventually follow Jesus on his journey to the Father, indeed he is going ahead to prepare a place for them (v. 2). Meanwhile, they are not left desolate. They have the privilege of knowing who Jesus is, even if that knowledge is partial and in need of refinement (v. 9). This knowledge empowers them to engage in the same works that they have witnessed Jesus perform, indeed they will engage in even greater works (v. 12).

The fact that Jesus imparts private 'knowledge' to his disciples has given rise to the claim that John's Gospel is perhaps the 'father of Gnosticism'. A number of variants on mainstream Christianity developed in the late first century at a time when Christian doctrine was developing. Many of these depended on the claim that the adherents were in possession of 'secret knowledge' imparted at initiation and derived from the hidden teachings of Jesus. A number of secret sayings of Jesus circulated and were eventually published as 'gnostic Gospels'. Most of these were suppressed by the later Church, but a number have recently come to light and may have been inspired by the private teaching of Jesus such as we find in this section of John's Gospel. What they have in common is a body of teaching about how the disciple might overcome the present troubles of this world.

The troubles that the disciples will encounter are elaborated in later chapters of John. The aim of this chapter is to give total reassurance to the disciples about the sort of 'aftercare' they can expect from the 'Counsellor' or the 'Spirit of truth whom the Father will send' (v. 16) in place of Jesus. The fact that this 'Counsellor' is a legal term for an advocate is a further indication of the sort of problems that the disciples will encounter as trouble brews with the local synagogue and the Roman authorities. As to the identity of this 'Counsellor', we are left in the dark. The fact that he is the 'Spirit of truth' may indicate that he is the presence of Jesus in another form; Jesus has already described himself as 'the way, the truth and the life' (v. 6).

The question of identity is introduced in this chapter when Philip asks Jesus to show them the Father. Jesus, with characteristic confidence, assures them that anyone who has seen him 'has seen the Father' (v. 9). Of course, the verb 'to see' means to perceive with a degree of spiritual discernment that even the disciples are not always capable of (v. 9).

The insight and assurances that Jesus shares with his followers are not just the result of privileged knowledge but a result of clear-sightedness. The concept of the body of Christ being the new community of believers will become a reality when they are able to see the issues as clearly as Jesus. The reason for this clear-sightedness is nothing to do with Jesus inhabiting that heavenly realm from the beginning of time, but rather because he has an unrestricted view of the Father, such is his trust and confidence in the Father. The promise made to Nathanael about an open heaven (1.51) was based on Jesus' own experience and insight. The Father has made himself known in and through Jesus because he is a faithful and obedient witness to the love of God (v. 21).

There is no doubt that this is one of the most confusing chapters in John's Gospel. We can almost imagine the disciples yawning and scratching during the course of what has become known as 'the long discourse'. In fact, by chapter 16, there is a minor protest when the disciples mutter that they 'do not understand what he is saying' (16.18). We might sympathize with Thomas, Philip and the other Judas, who fail to comprehend what Jesus is saying to them now, but when the Counsellor comes, all will be made plain (v. 26). These words of Jesus will be revealed and clarified by the passage of time. It is through the process of contemplative recall that this Gospel has come into being. The chapter ends with another assurance of protection and inner peace for those who believe. Although Jesus cannot be apprehended yet, the disciples must move on as the prince of this world approaches (v. 31). Jesus continues to be elusive for a little longer.

- **What sort of 'farewell speech' might a revered leader compose or have composed today?**
- **Do we have such leadership in Church or State today?**
- **What does the concept of a 'Paraclete' or 'Counsellor' mean for an understanding of the message of Jesus?**
- **How might we be led into the remembrance of the words of Jesus?**

30

Life Together in Terms of a Vine

John 15.1—16.4

[1]"I am the true vine, and my Father is the gardener. [2]He cuts off every branch in me that bears no fruit, while every branch that does bear fruit he prunes so that it will be even more fruitful. [3]You are already clean because of the word I have spoken to you. [4]Remain in me, and I will remain in you. No branch can bear fruit by itself; it must remain in the vine. Neither can you bear fruit unless you remain in me.

[5]I am the vine; you are the branches. If a man remains in me and I in him, he will bear much fruit; apart from me you can do nothing. [6]If anyone does not remain in me, he is like a branch that is thrown away and withers; such branches are picked up, thrown into the fire and burned. [7]If you remain in me and my words remain in you, ask whatever you wish, and it will be given you. [8]This is to my Father's glory, that you bear much fruit, showing yourselves to be my disciples.

[9]As the Father has loved me, so have I loved you. Now remain in my love. [10]If you obey my commands, you will remain in my love, just as I have obeyed my Father's commands and remain in his love. [11]I have told you this so that my joy may be in you and that your joy may be complete. [12]My command is this: Love each other as I have loved you. [13]Greater love has no-one than this, that he lay down his life for his friends. [14]You are my friends if you do what I command. [15]I no longer call you servants, because a servant does not know his master's business. Instead, I have called you friends, for everything that I learned from my Father I have made known to you. [16]You did not choose me, but I chose you and appointed you to go and bear fruit— fruit that will last. Then the Father will give you whatever you ask in my name. [17]This is my command: Love each other.

[18]If the world hates you, keep in mind that it hated me first. [19]If you belonged to the world, it would love you as its own. As it is, you do not belong to the world, but I have chosen you out of the world. That is why the world hates you. [20]Remember the words I spoke to you: "No servant is greater than his master." If they persecuted me, they will persecute you also. If they obeyed my teaching, they will obey yours also. [21]They will treat you this way because of my name, for they do not know the One who sent me. [22]If I had not come and spoken to them, they would not be guilty of sin. Now, however, they have no excuse for their sin. [23]He who hates me hates my Father as well. [24]If I had not done among them what no-one else did, they would not be guilty of sin. But now they have seen these miracles, and yet they have hated both me

and my Father. ²⁵But this is to fulfil what is written in their Law: "They hated me without reason."

²⁶'When the Counsellor comes, whom I will send to you from the Father, the Spirit of truth who goes out from the Father, he will testify about me. ²⁷And you also must testify, for you have been with me from the beginning.

^{16:1}'All this I have told you so that you will not go astray. ²They will put you out of the synagogue; in fact, a time is coming when anyone who kills you will think he is offering a service to God. ³They will do such things because they have not known the Father or me. ⁴I have told you this, so that when the time comes you will remember that I warned you. I did not tell you this at first because I was with you.

This chapter is about solidarity. A common theme through all the four Gospels is discipleship defined in terms of being 'with Jesus'. John gives that concept clarity and meaning in this famous chapter, which describes the relationship with Jesus both as organic (the vine) and as friendship based on love. True disciples are those with the gift of constancy. They need to 'remain' in the vine and bear fruit (vv. 5, 8, 9 and 16).

It is well known that John does not contain any of the parables that we find in the other Gospels. However, in this passage on the vine, we come close to the sort of word-picture that we met in chapter 10 on the 'good shepherd'.

Both the vine and the good shepherd images illuminate much of the teaching of this Gospel and help our understanding of the relationship between Jesus and his followers. The vine is a well-used image of the care that God lavishes on his people in the Old Testament. Isaiah 5 and Jeremiah 2.21 are the best-known examples. In both these passages the well-tended vine is unfruitful and deserving of harsh treatment. John's presentation concentrates on the need for pruning both to cut out the dead wood and to 'cleanse' (v. 2) the rest so that it may bear more fruit. Palestinian vineyards required patient tending. It might be up to three years before any fruit could be expected. It is obvious that growth in discipleship depended on patient viniculture by the gardener (God) and remaining grafted into the main stock (Jesus). Tending or 'cleansing' has already been dealt with in the feet-washing incident in chapter 13. By implication, those who have broken away from the main stock are neither clean nor capable of bearing fruit and therefore have forfeited their right to inherit life. Judas represents this sort of errant disciple. Possibly he is being used by John as a reminder to his first readers that the worst thing that could happen is for a disciple to break away from the close fellowship they experience as part of the 'vine'.

In order to sustain this solidarity, the disciple is encouraged to follow the example of Jesus, who inspires his followers to love one another in the way he has loved them. The proof of that love is demonstrated by Jesus in the sacrificial laying down of his life for them who are no longer described as disciples or sheep but as 'friends' (v. 13). So the link is established between this chapter with its use of the vine image and that of chapter 10 when the good shepherd is said to lay down his life for the sheep (v. 11). The relationship between the shepherd and his sheep is one of protection and care. That has now developed into a covenant relationship of reciprocal love and friendship between the shepherd and his sheep. This is the central theme of the rest of the 'farewell discourse'. The section began with a reference to the love Jesus had for the disciples (13.1). It will conclude with Jesus praying that 'the love with which the Father had for him may be in the disciples and he in them' (17.26). They are chosen for the purpose of bearing fruit which will last. They are to be the abiding testimony to the teachings of Jesus. This concept of indwelling in the mind of Jesus and being privy to the words of the Father is very like the thinking in Paul's letter to the Philippians where he encourages his readers to have the mind of Christ (Philippians 2.4).

This section on the importance of the love commandment ends with warnings about the cost of such love. Jesus has already demonstrated the length to which he is willing to go in order to express his love for the disciple. We have seen the opposition of the authorities resulting in expulsion from the synagogue for the man born blind; now Jesus warns the disciples to expect the same fate (v. 20 and 16.2). Jesus is presented in full prophetic mode, conveying to the disciples the words of God concerning the future which is now a present reality to the first readers of this Gospel.

- How is the commandment to love best put into effect?

- What is the difference between a sect and the sort of solidarity that is expected of the disciples in this passage?

- What sort of persecutions do you envisage happening to the first readers of this Gospel as a result of them being expelled from the synagogue?

- Can you think of any parallels to this situation in more recent history?

31

Jesus Talks Plainly to the Disciples

John 16.5–33

⁵"Now I am going to him who sent me, yet none of you asks me, "Where are you going?" ⁶Because I have said these things, you are filled with grief. ⁷But I tell you the truth: It is for your good that I am going away. Unless I go away, the Counsellor will not come to you; but if I go, I will send him to you. ⁸When he comes, he will convict the world of guilt in regard to sin and righteousness and judgment: ⁹in regard to sin, because men do not believe in me; ¹⁰in regard to righteousness, because I am going to the Father, where you can see me no longer; ¹¹and in regard to judgment, because the prince of this world now stands condemned.

¹²"I have much more to say to you, more than you can now bear. ¹³But when he, the Spirit of truth, comes, he will guide you into all truth. He will not speak on his own; he will speak only what he hears, and he will tell you what is yet to come. ¹⁴He will bring glory to me by taking from what is mine and making it known to you. ¹⁵All that belongs to the Father is mine. That is why I said the Spirit will take from what is mine and make it known to you.

¹⁶"In a little while you will see me no more, and then after a little while you will see me.'

¹⁷Some of his disciples said to one another, 'What does he mean by saying, "In a little while you will see me no more, and then after a little while you will see me," and "Because I am going to the Father"?' ¹⁸They kept asking, 'What does he mean by "a little while"? We don't understand what he is saying.'

¹⁹Jesus saw that they wanted to ask him about this, so he said to them, 'Are you asking one another what I meant when I said, "In a little while you will see me no more, and then after a little while you will see me"? ²⁰I tell you the truth, you will weep and mourn while the world rejoices. You will grieve, but your grief will turn to joy. ²¹A woman giving birth to a child has pain because her time has come; but when her baby is born she forgets the anguish because of her joy that a child is born into the world. ²²So with you: Now is your time of grief, but I will see you again and you will rejoice, and no-one will take away your joy. ²³In that day you will no longer ask me anything. I tell you the truth, my Father will give you whatever you ask in my name. ²⁴Until now you have not asked for anything in my name. Ask and you will receive, and your joy will be complete.

²⁵"Though I have been speaking figuratively, a time is coming when I will no longer use this kind of language but will tell you plainly about my Father. ²⁶In that day you will ask in my name. I am not saying that I will ask the Father

on your behalf. ²⁷No, the Father himself loves you because you have loved me and have believed that I came from God. ²⁸I came from the Father and entered the world; now I am leaving the world and going back to the Father.' ²⁹Then Jesus' disciples said, 'Now you are speaking clearly and without figures of speech. ³⁰Now we can see that you know all things and that you do not even need to have anyone ask you questions. This makes us believe that you came from God.' ³¹'You believe at last!' Jesus answered. ³²'But a time is coming, and has come, when you will be scattered, each to his own home. You will leave me all alone. Yet I am not alone, for my Father is with me.

³³'I have told you these things, so that in me you may have peace. In this world you will have trouble. But take heart! I have overcome the world.'

This chapter seeks to console the disciples in terms similar to those of chapter 14. Then Jesus had warned of a betrayal from within their own circle; now he has indicated the ferocity of the persecution they will experience from their own neighbours and kinsmen as a result of their beliefs. It is well known that a stiffening of resolve took place against the Christian movement as Jewish Councils began to regard them as blasphemers. To have been warned was a way of guarding against the breakdown of their faith. It is important that Jesus is seen to prepare them for each eventuality, as he is about to leave them in order to return to the one who sent him on this mission. The odd thing to note is the reticence of the disciples to intervene and ask Jesus about his mission and how it will affect them when they are abandoned. Jesus rebukes them for their silence in verse 5. (In fact we have not heard from them since chapter 14.) Despite this reprimand two of the disciples have asked him where he is going and received short shrift by way of an answer. Perhaps they have learnt not to ask Jesus too many questions. They admit as much in verse 30.

The consolation comes from the promise of the 'Counsellor' (v. 7) who will act as an advocate at the time of trial that they are to endure. In fact, the Spirit will speak on their behalf and convince the world of sin, righteousness and judgement (v. 8). Hence their faith will be strengthened. Although we have here the language of the Last Judgement, there is a strong sense in which this judgement is already taking place not only in the life and teaching of Jesus but also in the present experience of the readers of this Gospel. As so often for John, 'now is the hour of judgement for this world' (12.31).

Unlike the other Gospels, John does not present the disciples with a catalogue of woes about the last days. In fact he declines to burden them with too much detailed knowledge about the birth pangs of the new age. He is more concerned to give them a word picture which would assure them that the anguish will only be temporary, their sorrow will soon be turned to joy (v. 22). They have the reassurance that the Spirit will continue to interpret and clarify what is happening (v. 14). The disciples protest among themselves that they do not understand some of what Jesus is saying. The talk about his coming and going is particularly confusing. There is a comic moment in the drama when a stage whisper gets so loud that Jesus is forced to take notice (v. 19). Soon after this Jesus makes an important disclosure. No longer elusive he reveals his trump card and tells the disciples plainly that he has come from the Father and is returning to the Father (v. 28). Although Jesus had talked many times of going to the Father, he had never been properly understood. Now the penny seems to have dropped and the disciples declare that they fully understand Jesus' meaning (v. 30). This is akin to the transfiguration response we find in the other Gospels, when at least some of the inner circle have a momentary glimpse of who Jesus is and from where he originates. As with that story there now follows an immediate anti-climax for the disciples. The birth pangs Jesus has warned of are about to take place. The pain and joy that this represents is about to happen. Jesus too will experience a death in order that a new birth might take place. Likewise, the disciples will suffer the pain and shame of deserting Jesus. But they are not to be crushed by this sorrow. As Jesus says, 'In the world you will have tribulation; but be of good cheer, I have overcome the world' (v. 33). This is the assurance that Jesus provides not only to the assembled disciples but also to the the early Church which is addressed through them.

- **In what form do you think the Spirit may be said to take the words of Jesus and declare them to the disciples?**
- **Is this passage a fair description of what is happening throughout John's Gospel?**
- **How clear is it to you what Jesus says of himself in John?**
- **Do you think this is a clearer presentation than that found elsewhere in the New Testament?**

JESUS IS LIFTED UP

32

The Prayer of Jesus

John 17.1–26

¹**After Jesus said this, he looked towards heaven and prayed:**

'Father, the time has come. Glorify your Son, that your Son may glorify you. ²For you granted him authority over all people that he might give eternal life to all those you have given him. ³Now this is eternal life: that they may know you, the only true God, and Jesus Christ, whom you have sent. ⁴I have brought you glory on earth by completing the work you gave me to do. ⁵And now, Father, glorify me in your presence with the glory I had with you before the world began.

⁶'I have revealed you to those whom you gave me out of the world. They were yours; you gave them to me and they have obeyed your word. ⁷Now they know that everything you have given me comes from you. ⁸For I gave them the words you gave me and they accepted them. They knew with certainty that I came from you, and they believed that you sent me. ⁹I pray for them. I am not praying for the world, but for those you have given me, for they are yours. ¹⁰All I have is yours, and all you have is mine. And glory has come to me through them. ¹¹I will remain in the world no longer, but they are still in the world, and I am coming to you. Holy Father, protect them by the power of your name—the name you gave me—so that they may be one as we are one. ¹²While I was with them, I protected them and kept them safe by that name you gave me. None has been lost except the one doomed to destruction so that Scripture would be fulfilled.

¹³'I am coming to you now, but I say these things while I am still in the world, so that they may have the full measure of my joy within them. ¹⁴I have given them your word and the world has hated them, for they are not of the world any more than I am of the world. ¹⁵My prayer is not that you take them out of the world but that you protect them from the evil one. ¹⁶They are not of the world, even as I am not of it. ¹⁷Sanctify them by the truth; your word is truth. ¹⁸As you sent me

into the world, I have sent them into the world. [19]For them I sanctify myself, that they too may be truly sanctified. [20]'My prayer is not for them alone. I pray also for those who will believe in me through their message, [21]that all of them may be one, Father, just as you are in me and I am in you. May they also be in us so that the world may believe that you have sent me. [22]I have given them the glory that you gave me, that they may be one as we are one: [23]I in them and you in me. May they be brought to complete unity to let the world know that you sent me and have loved them even as you have loved me. [24]'Father, I want those you have given me to be with me where I am, and to see my glory, the glory you have given me because you loved me before the creation of the world. [25]'Righteous Father, though the world does not know you, I know you, and they know that you have sent me. [26]I have made you known to them, and will continue to make you known in order that the love you have for me may be in them and that I myself may be in them.'

We are now nearing the completion of this section of Jesus' long farewell discourse with his disciples in which he has prepared them to face both his own suffering and theirs. He now turns to the Father in prayer. According to the other Gospels, the same thing happens in the Garden of Gethsemane. Whereas that prayer agonized about the suffering to come, this prayer is confident in the completion of a task well done in accordance with the Father's wishes. The prayer is a 'last will and testament' in which Jesus commits the disciples into the protection of the Father. Again the image of the good shepherd and the vine lie behind the text. The good shepherd, about to lay down his life for the sheep, stands at the entrance of the olive grove praying for those who are bound up with him and his mission, for without their continuing work in the world that mission will be in jeopardy.

As in the Gethsemane prayer of the other Gospels, this prayer has echoes of what we know as the 'Lord's Prayer', for instance, 'keep them from the evil one' (v. 15). Presented as a perfect submission to the Father's will, this prayer sees the crucifixion less in terms of a cup of suffering than as 'glorification' (v. 1). Eternal life in this prayer is understood to result from the knowledge of God and Jesus whom he has sent to reveal him on the cross (v. 3). The prayer is only possible because the disciples have, at last, fully benefited from the teaching of the last four chapters. They have made the declaration that they know where Jesus comes from. The first followers, in chapter 1, were invited to 'come and see' where Jesus was staying. They could not have realized then that the place where Jesus resides is in the bosom of the Father (1.18). Now, because they are learning to dwell in his love, they too are to share in the heavenly dwelling-place. Jesus prays that they might enjoy the same intimacy that he has by abiding in the Father's presence. The prayer for the unity of the disciples is not for some united ecumenical movement, important though unity is among Christians. The prayer is for the members of the 'vine' that they might fully be bonded into a common fellowship with the Father; the same union that the Father and the Son have experienced from the beginning.

As with the transfiguration scene in the other Gospels, Jesus is caught up in a glorified state so that he appears to be both apart from this world and yet still within it. In fact Jesus is on the first leg of a heavenly journey. Like some cosmic time traveller, Jesus is suspended some way between 'this-worldly' experience and that of another heavenly realm. The next stage of this journey will involve him physically suspended between heaven and earth when he is lifted up on the cross. Meanwhile the reader, like the disciple, is invited to overhear the intimate conversation between the Father and the Son. What we are witnessing in this chapter is the beginnings of an 'open heaven'; the fulfilment of the promise made to Nathanael in chapter 1.

- Why do the evangelists describe the prayers of Jesus in this way when it is obvious that such prayers could not have been overheard by anyone?

- This 'Prayer of Jesus' is not a prayer in the ordinary sense of the word. It is a further example of how John presents Jesus as a heavenly revealer. How important is this picture in John's Gospel?

- There are a number of references to the 'world' in this chapter (vv. 7, 11, 13, 14, 15, 16, 18). What is Jesus' attitude to the 'world' as it is described in John?

33

Jesus is Handed Over

John 18.1–27

¹**When he had finished praying, Jesus left** with his disciples and crossed the Kidron Valley. On the other side there was an olive grove, and he and his disciples went into it. ²Now Judas, who betrayed him, knew the place, because Jesus had often met there with his disciples. ³So Judas came to the grove, guiding a detachment of soldiers and some officials from the chief priests and Pharisees. They were carrying torches, lanterns and weapons.

⁴Jesus, knowing all that was going to happen to him, went out and asked them, 'Who is it you want?'

⁵'Jesus of Nazareth,' they replied.

'I am he,' Jesus said. (And Judas the traitor was standing there with them.) ⁶When Jesus said, 'I am he,' they drew back and fell to the ground.

⁷Again he asked them, 'Who is it you want?' And they said, 'Jesus of Nazareth.'

⁸'I told you that I am he,' Jesus answered. 'If you are looking for me, then let these men go.' ⁹This happened so that the words he had spoken would be fulfilled: 'I have not lost one of those you gave me.'

¹⁰Then Simon Peter, who had a sword, drew it and struck the high priest's servant, cutting off his right ear. (The servant's name was Malchus.)

¹¹Jesus commanded Peter, 'Put your sword away! Shall I not drink the cup the Father has given me?'

¹²Then the detachment of soldiers with its commander and the Jewish officials arrested Jesus. They bound him ¹³and brought him first to Annas, who was the father-in-law of Caiaphas, the high priest that year. ¹⁴Caiaphas was the one who had advised the Jews that it would be good if one man died for the people.

¹⁵Simon Peter and another disciple were following Jesus. Because this disciple was known to the high priest, he went with Jesus into the high priest's courtyard, ¹⁶but Peter had to wait outside at the door. The other disciple, who was known to the high priest, came back, spoke to the girl on duty there and brought Peter in.

¹⁷'You are not one of his disciples, are you?' the girl at the door asked Peter.

He replied, 'I am not.'

¹⁸It was cold, and the servants and officials stood round a fire they had made to keep warm. Peter also was standing with them, warming himself.

¹⁹Meanwhile, the high priest questioned Jesus about his disciples and his teaching.

²⁰'I have spoken openly to the world,' Jesus replied. 'I always taught in synagogues or at the temple, where all the Jews come together.

I said nothing in secret. ²¹Why question me? Ask those who heard me. Surely they know what I said.' ²²When Jesus said this, one of the officials near by struck him in the face. 'Is this the way you answer the high priest?' he demanded. ²³'If I said something wrong,' Jesus replied, 'testify as to what is wrong. But if I spoke the truth, why did you strike me?' ²⁴Then Annas sent him, still bound, to Caiaphas the high priest.

²⁵As Simon Peter stood warming himself, he was asked, 'You are not one of his disciples, are you?' He denied it, saying, 'I am not.' ²⁶One of the high priest's servants, a relative of the man whose ear Peter had cut off, challenged him, 'Didn't I see you with him in the olive grove?' ²⁷Again Peter denied it, and at that moment a cock began to crow.

After a long discussion with the disciples in chapters 14—17, we now come to the dramatic climax of the Gospel in which John relates to us his understanding of the events that lead up to the death and resurrection of Jesus (18—19). Some scholars have noted the links between the form of John's Gospel and that of Greek tragedy. Nowhere is this more evident than in these chapters. This passage sets the tone; the farewell speeches being concluded, the action immediately starts up again. Like some tragic hero who is fully aware of his fate (v. 4), Jesus sets out with his disciples to cross the Kidron Valley (v. 1). As with every reference in John's Gospel there is more than a simple interest in geographic or historical detail. In mentioning the name of this wadi between the city of Jerusalem and the garden of Gethsemane (which is not named), John is again teasing us with a series of clues and cross-references. In translation the word 'Kidron' has something to do with darkness. The darkness is continually emphasized in this section. Jesus is seen as 'the light of the world' and the forces of darkness attempt to extinguish that light as was foretold in the prologue (1.5). We are also reminded of the resolution of Jesus in the other Gospels in setting his face to what awaited him in this city.

By omitting to mention 'Gethsemane', John draws attention to the word 'garden'. This reminds us of two other gardens; that of Eden and that of the resurrection. This garden is deemed to be a 'safe place' as the disciples, we are told, often met there (v. 2). Is John alluding to his image of Jesus as the 'good shepherd'? There are a number of allusions in the text to suggest this: the garden may indeed be walled and resemble a sheepfold; Jesus appears to stand at the entrance and defend his own from attack; Judas approaches as a thief ready to harry the flock. John may be presenting the courtyard of the high priest as another sheepfold; a place from which Peter, in the role of a 'hireling', runs away (10.12–13).

There is no doubt that Jesus fulfils the role of the tragic hero in this story, yet a hero who is completely in control of the events. A huge detachment of soldiers (some 600) arrive to arrest Jesus with the aid of lanterns. John again stresses the irony of the situation: those with the eyes of faith would not need light to see the true light. When they arrive they are interrogated by the one they have come to arrest. He asks them cryptically, 'Whom do you seek?' (vv. 4 and 7). We are reminded of the first words of Jesus in chapter 1 (v. 38) and his first words to Mary Magdalene in the Easter garden (20.15). In using the 'I am' formula Jesus is seen to have some kind of divine authority which even these soldiers recognize as they fall to the ground in his presence (v. 6). There is no need for Judas to identify Jesus with the famous kiss. In John Jesus makes his own self-disclosure. In the struggle which follows, Peter attacks a senior member of the high priest's household. This shows Peter in a bad light. From now on he is contrasted with the way Jesus conducts himself. Although he is said to 'follow' Jesus with the unnamed disciple (v. 15), he is hardly portrayed as a model disciple. His behaviour in the courtyard, when he repeatedly denies his knowledge of Jesus, is a foil to the open testimony that Jesus offers in the room above. A fourteenth-century painting of this scene by Duccio makes the link by joining both scenes by means of a staircase. Peter, like Judas in the garden, is described as 'standing' with the representatives of the world opposed to the light that Jesus represents. It is in this courtyard that he hears the cock crow; but we are not told that he draws any significance from that event. Standing with the world Peter is both deaf and blind to what is happening. This situation will not be resolved until we reach chapter 21, when an attempt is made to reinstate Peter.

• **Notice the repeated references to the darkness and the cold in this passage. Can both Judas and Peter be allied to these concepts?**

- How much are we out in the dark in respect to understanding Jesus and what he represents?

- Peter is reinstated in chapter 21. Why is it that Judas is given harsher treatment in this Gospel?

- What sort of leadership is the 'good shepherd' offering? Is it a viable alternative to that displayed by high priests?

34

Disclosures Before Pilate

John 18.28—19.22

²⁸**Then the Jews led Jesus from Caiaphas** to the palace of the Roman governor. By now it was early morning, and to avoid ceremonial uncleanness the Jews did not enter the palace; they wanted to be able to eat the Passover. ²⁹So Pilate came out to them and asked, 'What charges are you bringing against this man?' ³⁰'If he were not a criminal,' they replied, 'we would not have handed him over to you.' ³¹Pilate said, 'Take him yourselves and judge him by your own law.'

'But we have no right to execute anyone,' the Jews objected. ³²This happened so that the words Jesus had spoken indicating the kind of death he was going to die would be fulfilled.

³³Pilate then went back inside the palace, summoned Jesus and asked him, 'Are you the king of the Jews?'

³⁴'Is that your own idea,' Jesus asked, 'or did others talk to you about me?'

³⁵'Am I a Jew?' Pilate replied. 'It was your people and your chief priests who handed you over to me. What is it you have done?'

³⁶Jesus said, 'My kingdom is not of this world. If it were, my servants would fight to prevent my arrest by the Jews. But now my kingdom is from another place.'

³⁷'You are a king, then!' said Pilate.

Jesus answered, 'You are right in saying I am a king. In fact, for this reason I was born, and for this I came into the world, to testify to the truth. Everyone on the side of truth listens to me.'

³⁸'What is truth?' Pilate asked. With this he went out again to the Jews and said, 'I find no basis for a charge against him. ³⁹But it is your custom for me to release to you one prisoner at the time of the Passover. Do you want me to release "the king of the Jews"?'

⁴⁰They shouted back, 'No, not him! Give us Barabbas!' Now Barabbas had taken part in a rebellion.

¹⁹:¹Then Pilate took Jesus and had him flogged. ²The soldiers twisted together a crown of thorns and put it on his head. They clothed him in a purple robe ³and went up to him again and again, saying, 'Hail, king of the Jews!' And they struck him in the face.

⁴Once more Pilate came out and said to the Jews, 'Look, I am bringing him out to you to let you know that I find no basis for a charge against him.' ⁵When Jesus came out wearing the crown of thorns and the purple robe, Pilate said to them, 'Here is the man!'

⁶As soon as the chief priests and their officials saw him, they shouted, 'Crucify! Crucify!'

But Pilate answered, 'You take him and crucify him. As for me, I find no basis for a charge against him.'

⁷The Jews insisted, 'We have a law, and according to that law he must die, because he claimed to be the Son of God.'

⁸When Pilate heard this, he was even more afraid, ⁹and he went back inside the palace. 'Where do you come from?' he asked Jesus, but Jesus gave him no answer. ¹⁰'Do you refuse to speak to me?' Pilate said. 'Don't you realise I have power either to free you or to crucify you?'

¹¹Jesus answered, 'You would have no power over me if it were not given to you from above. Therefore the one who handed me over to you is guilty of a greater sin.'

¹²From then on, Pilate tried to set Jesus free, but the Jews kept shouting, 'If you let this man go, you are no friend of Caesar. Anyone who claims to be a king opposes Caesar.'

¹³When Pilate heard this, he brought Jesus out and sat down on the judge's seat at a place known as the Stone Pavement (which in Aramaic is Gabbatha). ¹⁴It was the day of Preparation of Passover Week, about the sixth hour.

'Here is your king,' Pilate said to the Jews.

¹⁵But they shouted, 'Take him away! Take him away! Crucify him!'

'Shall I crucify your king?' Pilate asked.

'We have no king but Caesar,' the chief priests answered.

¹⁶Finally Pilate handed him over to them to be crucified.

So the soldiers took charge of Jesus. ¹⁷Carrying his own cross, he went out to the place of the Skull (which in Aramaic is called Golgotha). ¹⁸Here they crucified him, and with him two others—one on each side and Jesus in the middle.

¹⁹Pilate had a notice prepared and fastened to the cross. It read: JESUS OF NAZARETH, THE KING OF THE JEWS. ²⁰Many of the Jews read this sign, for the place where Jesus was crucified was near the city, and the sign was written in Aramaic, Latin and Greek. ²¹The chief priests of the Jews protested to Pilate, 'Do not write "The King of the Jews", but that this man claimed to be king of the Jews.'

²²Pilate answered, 'What I have written, I have written.'

Having been interrogated and roughed up by the religious authorities, Jesus now appears before the secular powers on a criminal charge. It has to be repeated that John's purpose is not to present a historically accurate account of these trials, but to reveal the theological implications of what took place and to relate them to recent events and concerns within his own community, where the big issue was relations with Judaism and the Roman state. These two trials provide the perfect forum for establishing the emerging Christian Church's relationship to these two major institutions; the sacred and the secular. John, more than the other Gospels, emphasizes the criminal and political nature of the charges. This Gospel was written at a time when the status of Christianity was in question. Some Jews regarded it as a heretical Jewish sect, others as a subversive political movement. So it was important for John to provide a good defence of Jesus as the inspiration of those who, at the time of writing, were suffering similar intimidations. The whole of this section is based on interpretation rather than fact. No eye witness could have been present at the numerous comings and goings of Pilate and the private conversations between him and Jesus. However, the style may be likened to that of modern literary fiction in which the author gets very close to the tenor of the events by weaving a dialogue around known facts.

John has long been recognized as containing a number of accurate historical references which add to the verisimilitude of his Gospel. Within this chapter he has accurately reported that Annas was the father-in-law of Caiaphas and that the Jews had no powers to impose capital punishment. Other details about family ties between Malchus and a bystander, and the 'beloved' disciple's connections, all have a ring of probability about them. John has a habit of scattering clues around which indicate that his source may be as close or even closer to the actual events than the other Gospels. But as he reminds us at the end of the Gospel (21.25), his purpose is not to provide a chronicle but a selection to encourage belief (20.31). The characterization of Pilate is dealt with elsewhere. All we need note is that Jesus is not silent, as he is in the other accounts. Here he takes control of the discussion and supplies Pilate with enough clues for him to realize that he is in the presence of something more than a common criminal. The storytelling is as gripping as something from a Beckett or a Pinter play. The one who appears to have power loses it in the presence of one who appears to be powerless. The 'truth' about which Pilate is so sceptical is staring him in the face (v. 38). Sadly, neither he nor the Jews perceive this. The crowds scream for Barabbas (v. 40) while the true son of the Father remains unrecognized, for 'he came to his own and his own received him not' (1.11).

In presenting Jesus as a mock king (v. 39), Pilate inflames the crowd, who bay for his blood, thereby rejecting their true king for a foreign despot (v. 15). The irony is that the Passover hymn soon to be sung expressly states that there is no king but God. Spiritual blindness is given a further dramatic twist. The drama continues with Pilate attempting to appease the Jews by having Jesus scourged (v. 1). The soldiers' treatment and their 'regal mockery' only inflames the crowds and they again fail to see their true king, who is a man in the tradition of Daniel's 'Son of Man', who represents the persecuted saints of the Most High. This king is like no other in history. The rejection is final and complete.

The narrative is given a further dramatic twist as Pilate eventually betrays his own instincts and 'delivers up' Jesus to be crucified (19.16). Now the 'king' is led away to be raised up and nailed naked on a wooden throne. Before this is achieved, Pilate is caught up in one last act of irony. He unwittingly proclaims to the world in three languages the truth he failed to recognize: 'Jesus of Nazareth King of the Jews' (v. 19).

- If Jesus was arrested on a political charge today, would he receive a similar form of treatment?

- Why is it, do you think, that Jesus is silent about his origins?

- Why do you think Pilate felt intimidated by Jesus? What is John's purpose in presenting this picture of a vacillating governor?

- Why is Pilate so adamant about what he has written on the notice above the cross?

35

The King must Die

John 19.23–42

²³**When the soldiers crucified Jesus, they** took his clothes, dividing them into four shares, one for each of them, with the undergarment remaining. This garment was seamless, woven in one piece from top to bottom.

²⁴'Let's not tear it,' they said to one another. 'Let's decide by lot who will get it.'

This happened that the scripture might be fulfilled which said,

'They divided my garments among
   them and cast lots for my clothing.'

So this is what the soldiers did.

²⁵Near the cross of Jesus stood his mother, his mother's sister, Mary the wife of Clopas, and Mary Magdalene. ²⁶When Jesus saw his mother there, and the disciple whom he loved standing near by, he said to his mother, 'Dear woman, here is your son,' ²⁷and to the disciple, 'Here is your mother.' From that time on, this disciple took her into his home.

²⁸Later, knowing that all was now completed, and so that the Scripture would be fulfilled, Jesus said, 'I am thirsty.' ²⁹A jar of wine vinegar was there, so they soaked a sponge in it, put the sponge on a stalk of the hyssop plant, and lifted it to Jesus' lips. ³⁰When he had received the drink, Jesus said, 'It is finished.' With that, he bowed his head and gave up his spirit.

³¹Now it was the day of Preparation, and the next day was to be a special Sabbath. Because the Jews did not want the bodies left on the crosses during the Sabbath, they asked Pilate to have the legs broken and the bodies taken down. ³²The soldiers therefore came and broke the legs of the first man who had been crucified with Jesus, and then those of the other. ³³But when they came to Jesus and found that he was already dead, they did not break his legs. ³⁴Instead, one of the soldiers pierced Jesus' side with a spear, bringing a sudden flow of blood and water. ³⁵The man who saw it has given testimony, and his testimony is true. He knows that he tells the truth, and he testifies so that you also may believe. ³⁶These things happened so that the scripture would be fulfilled: 'Not one of his bones will be broken,' ³⁷and, as another scripture says, 'They will look on the one they have pierced.'

³⁸Later, Joseph of Arimathea asked Pilate for the body of Jesus. Now Joseph was a disciple of Jesus, but secretly because he feared the Jews. With Pilate's permission, he came and took the body away. ³⁹He was accompanied by Nicodemus, the man who earlier had visited Jesus at night. Nicodemus brought a mixture of myrrh and aloes, about seventy-five pounds. ⁴⁰Taking Jesus' body, the two of them wrapped it, with the spices, in strips of

linen. This was in accordance with Jewish burial customs. ⁴¹At the place where Jesus was crucified, there was a garden, and in the garden a new tomb, in which no-one had ever been laid. ⁴²Because it was the Jewish day of Preparation and since the tomb was near by, they laid Jesus there.

The description of the crucifixion is minimalist in all the Gospels. There is no attempt to describe the appalling horror of the execution; the text merely states that they crucified Jesus alongside two others (v. 18). For the writer of this Gospel this is the final and most significant signal that God is disclosing himself to the world in the most degrading and humiliating circumstances. The business of disclosure involves risk. In entrusting 'all things' to the Son (13.3) the Father has emptied himself of all power to coerce a response from his world. He simply surrenders himself in an act of total self-giving love; the same sort of 'kenotic' self-emptying that Paul speaks of in Philippians 2 and of which Jesus speaks to Nicodemus in 3.16.

What is described at length is the garments. The soldiers cast lots for the seamless robe (v. 24). This is the sort of vestment that the high priest would wear. John is again developing the irony for which he is famous. At the site of the crucifixion Jesus is proclaimed both priest and king to those with eyes to see. Sadly, there are few who would make this connection, except one perhaps. The beloved disciple stands at the foot of the cross, the only male disciple among so many women. We have already noted the perspicacity of the women in this Gospel. The beloved disciple stands alongside such, and is seen as the model disciple who remains loyal and devoted to Jesus.

One whose loyalty and devotion is not usually questioned is the mother of Jesus. She too stands at the foot of the cross in this Gospel. However, she is not mentioned in the others, not even in Luke, who is more ready than the others to pay Mary the respect that we are used to affording her as the mother of Jesus. There is a certain ambiguity in John as to how much Mary is seen as a disciple. Here she seems to represent that section of John's community who love and respect the memory of Jesus but as yet have not made the faith response by recognizing that he is the mouthpiece or 'Word' of God disclosing his nature and meaning to the world. Now that Jesus is seen to penetrate the heavens by being elevated between heaven and earth, he is the living ladder between these two spheres. He looks down at the two people who are the closest to him, and commends each to the other (v. 27). This may well be a coded message to his first readers to love and nurture those members of the community who for whatever reason have not yet come to a full understanding of the good news as he has related it.

The scene is concluded with a double reference to completion (vv. 28 and 30). Jesus has finished the work that the Father had commissioned him to fulfil. He can now surrender his spirit or the breath of God back to the Father. The death of Jesus is presented as a victory. Jesus has fully achieved his purpose in this the most desolate and macabre setting. The irony that requires the body of Jesus to be hastily removed, in case it should desecrate the approaching festival, is not lost on the readers of this Gospel. John has consistently presented Jesus as the substitution for the cult, either in the form of festival or temple. The body itself is not desecrated but left intact as a paschal lamb might be. Jesus, the 'Lamb of God' (1.29), dies at the same moment as the paschal lambs are slaughtered in the temple.

The testimony of the witness who saw these things happen helps verify the theology behind these events. The strange reference to the flow of water and blood from the side of the dead Jesus is a way of emphasizing that a new covenant is established between God and humanity in these events. Water is the means of baptism and new beginnings for the believer, and blood is required for a renewal of the covenant. The flow of water and blood is also reminiscent of the new birth that is referred to in 3.3 and 16.21.

Finally, the scene closes with the reappearance of Nicodemus in the company of Joseph of Arimathea, who is familiar to us by being mentioned in the other Gospels. Although fearful of the 'Jews', they pay their respects to the dead Jesus by providing a prodigious amount of aromatic oils with which to embalm his body. This royal treatment, alongside the burial in a new tomb, underlines the suggestion that this is a royal funeral. Jesus of Nazareth, the king of the Jews, has been laid to rest by two members of the Jewish ruling Council who, while respecting him, have, as yet, failed to recognize him.

- Why was it necessary for Jesus to die in this horrific and degrading manner?

- In what way can it be claimed that Jesus 'reigns from the tree' in John's Gospel?

- What expectations do you think Nicodemus and Joseph had of a new beginning?

- Does the crucifixion make sense of our understanding of sin and atonement?

36

Mary Sees the Lord

John 20.1–18

¹**Early on the first day of the week, while** it was still dark, Mary Magdalene went to the tomb and saw that the stone had been removed from the entrance. ²So she came running to Simon Peter and the other disciple, the one Jesus loved, and said, 'They have taken the Lord out of the tomb, and we don't know where they have put him!' ³So Peter and the other disciple started for the tomb. ⁴Both were running, but the other disciple outran Peter and reached the tomb first. ⁵He bent over and looked in at the strips of linen lying there but did not go in. ⁶Then Simon Peter, who was behind him, arrived and went into the tomb. He saw the strips of linen lying there, ⁷as well as the burial cloth that had been around Jesus' head. The cloth was folded up by itself, separate from the linen. ⁸Finally the other disciple, who had reached the tomb first, also went inside. He saw and believed. ⁹(They still did not understand from Scripture that Jesus had to rise from the dead.) ¹⁰Then the disciples went back to their homes, ¹¹but Mary stood outside the tomb crying. As she wept, she bent over to look into the tomb ¹²and saw two angels in white, seated where Jesus' body had been, one at the head and the other at the foot. ¹³They asked her, 'Woman, why are you crying?'

'They have taken my Lord away,' she said, 'and I don't know where they have put him.' ¹⁴At this, she turned round and saw Jesus standing there, but she did not realise that it was Jesus.

¹⁵'Woman,' he said, 'why are you crying? Who is it you are looking for?'

Thinking he was the gardener, she said, 'Sir, if you have carried him away, tell me where you have put him, and I will get him.' ¹⁶Jesus said to her, 'Mary.'

She turned towards him and cried out in Aramaic, 'Rabboni!' (which means Teacher). ¹⁷Jesus said, 'Do not hold on to me, for I have not yet returned to the Father. Go instead to my brothers and tell them, "I am returning to my Father and your Father, to my God and your God."'

¹⁸Mary Magdalene went to the disciples with the news: 'I have seen the Lord!' And she told them that he had said these things to her.

The last chapter ended with Jesus laid to rest in a new tomb. This chapter opens with Mary Magdalene approaching this tomb at the first possible opportunity after the Sabbath observance. We are not told the reason for this visit but are left to speculate that if she is the sister of Martha and Lazarus she has come to complete the task she set herself in chapter 12 when she began to anoint Jesus in preparation for his burial. She may have been perceptive then and was commended for it by Jesus, but now things are very different. Her hope and vision is clouded by grief. On approaching the tomb she discovers that the stone had been removed. She then runs and tells Peter and the beloved disciple what has happened. They both hurry to the tomb to find it as Mary describes, John arriving first. It is at this point that the game of seeking and finding moves into top gear. The beloved disciple peeps inside to see an array of linen but does not enter. Simon, however, blunders in and notes the carefully arranged linen. He is followed by the other disciple, who makes a kind of faith connection for he 'sees and believes' (v. 8).

The story is told with such relish and haste that we should be careful not to overlook the significance of the detail. Firstly, there is a lot about linen. Why, one might ask? Is this another example of John's verisimilitude, detail that makes the narrative come alive? Possibly, but I believe there is more to this than mere local colour. The grave linen is given prominence to emphasize that this is a resurrection not a resuscitation. Lazarus was revived. He came out bound from head to foot in grave clothes and had to be released (11.44). Jesus is raised by the power of God alone and needs no human assistance. If the beloved disciple is Lazarus, as some believe, then the significance of the grave clothes would not be lost on him and may be instrumental in his coming to faith.

The theme of 'hide and seek' is again rehearsed in the second part of this story. Mary stands weeping outside the tomb. If she is the sister of Lazarus then she and Jesus have wept before in similar circumstances in front of her brother's grave (11.33 ff.). Then she had fallen at the feet of Jesus (11.32) and had invited him to 'come and see' the tomb. If this is the same Mary, and I am convinced that it is, then the scene makes a lot more sense. What we have here is a recapitulation of the sign of the raising of Lazarus, when Jesus announced himself as 'the resurrection and the life'. What Mary is about to witness is the final sign of that truth having taken place. She will now fully understand what Jesus meant by describing himself as 'the resurrection and the life' (11.25). The raising of Lazarus had demonstrated the glory of God and the power of the resurrection life. It had also resulted in the plot to destroy Jesus, which Mary had understood. Now her understanding would be enlarged. She continues to seek for an answer to the question that many have asked in this Gospel. 'Where is Jesus?' The angels ask her why she weeps. The time for weeping has passed, but Mary, as yet, has not perceived this. Then Jesus himself asks the same question, 'Woman, why do you weep? Whom do you seek?' (v. 15). Having turned round as Jesus did in chapter 1, she does so again and this time is able to recognize Jesus not as the gardener as she first thought, but as her 'teacher' (v. 16), the word that Mary uses of Jesus in chapter 11. However, this time the word 'teacher' is given in its Hebrew form and is the title normally reserved for God as 'Rabboni'.

This remarkable passage ends with a commission to Mary to announce to the disciples that their Lord is not only risen – but ascending to his Father and to their Father (v. 17). Mary is the first apostle to deliver the good news to the male disciples that she has seen the Lord.

- **What is it that blinds the disciples to the fact that Jesus may be risen from the dead?**

- **What caused the beloved disciple to 'see and believe'?**

- **What part does Peter play in this drama? Would you say he has the same insight as the other two disciples mentioned in the text?**

- **What is the role of Mary Magdalene in the resurrection story? Why is she asked not to touch Jesus?**

- **Why do you think John makes a link between the resurrection and the ascension in this passage?**

'Written that You Might Believe'

John 20.19–31

¹⁹**On the evening of that first day of the week**, when the disciples were together, with the doors locked for fear of the Jews, Jesus came and stood among them and said, 'Peace be with you!' ²⁰After he said this, he showed them his hands and side. The disciples were overjoyed when they saw the Lord.

²¹Again Jesus said, 'Peace be with you! As the Father has sent me, I am sending you.' ²²And with that he breathed on them and said, 'Receive the Holy Spirit. ²³If you forgive anyone his sins, they are forgiven; if you do not forgive them, they are not forgiven.'

²⁴Now Thomas (called Didymus), one of the Twelve, was not with the disciples when Jesus came. ²⁵So the other disciples told him, 'We have seen the Lord!'

But he said to them, 'Unless I see the nail marks in his hands and put my finger where the nails were, and put my hand into his side, I will not believe it.'

²⁶A week later his disciples were in the house again, and Thomas was with them. Though the doors were locked, Jesus came and stood among them and said, 'Peace be with you!' ²⁷Then he said to Thomas, 'Put your finger here; see my hands. Reach out your hand and put it into my side. Stop doubting and believe.' ²⁸Thomas said to him, 'My Lord and my God!' ²⁹Then Jesus told him, 'Because you have seen me, you have believed; blessed are those who have not seen and yet have believed.'

³⁰Jesus did many other miraculous signs in the presence of his disciples, which are not recorded in this book. ³¹But these are written that you may believe that Jesus is the Christ, the Son of God, and that by believing you may have life in his name.

Mary had seen Jesus standing in the garden and had come to believe in him as the 'resurrection and the life'. The experience had transformed her sorrow into joy and she had been commissioned to stand before the other disciples and testify that she had seen the Lord. Jesus had spoken to his disciples about such experiences in chapter 16 (v. 22). The disciples are now to enjoy the same experience as Mary in that they too are to see him 'standing' among them later that same day. They may have heard the good news but, as yet, they are unable to act on it for they are still behind locked doors 'for fear of the Jews' (v. 19). Jesus appears and shares his peace with them not once but twice. The peace that Jesus assured them of in chapter 15 (v. 27) is given them by the risen Christ, who then breathes new life into his frightened disciples. This is a clear allusion to the life-giving breathing of God into Adam in the Genesis story (Genesis 2.7). They are receiving the Holy Spirit, the promised 'Counsellor' who was also mentioned in chapter 15 (v. 26). He it is who will testify on behalf of Jesus when the disciples find themselves ghettoized and in fear of the 'Jews'.

John's account differs from the presentation we find in Luke, who works with another timescale. In Luke the resurrection, ascension and giving of the Spirit is drawn out over a period of weeks. As we have just seen, John is concerned to present the death, resurrection, ascension and the coming of the Spirit as one continuous act. Jesus is elevated on the cross where he reigns as king and breathes out his spirit. At his resurrection he talks of his ascending to the Father, and later that day he breathes the Holy Spirit on his followers with the commission to forgive sins.

All the appearances have been difficult for the disciples. First, they have no expectation that Jesus will rise from the dead. When they are confronted with the risen Christ, initially they have problems recognizing him. This is a common feature of all the resurrection accounts in all the Gospels. It may indicate a perceived difference in the risen body from that of the earthly body; something that Paul discusses in 1 Corinthians 15. This inability to recognize Jesus is an illustration of the blindness foretold by Isaiah (6.10) and quoted by John in chapter 12 (v. 40). The need to 'turn and be healed' is demonstrated perfectly in the behaviour of Mary Magdalene who turns, not once but twice, in this account as she is healed of her desolation and grief.

One character who is told of the resurrection but refuses to believe without material proof is Thomas. He is used as a sort of 'stooge' to demonstrate the blessedness of those who come to faith without the benefit of sight. We are not told if he chose to accept the invitation to put his finger in the nail prints; it rather seems as if that was deemed unnecessary. In fact Thomas makes the most perfect faith response in the Gospel, confessing Jesus to be both his 'Lord' and his 'God' (v. 28).

The final beatitude is given to those who come to faith on the testimony of others. The evangelist closes the first draft of his Gospel by telling us that the reason for his writing it was that others may confess the faith that Thomas confesses; that they might believe even without seeing.

- Why is John presenting Easter to Pentecost as happening all on one day?

- If the resurrection accounts all differ, is this evidence for their veracity or their unreliability? Are the differences a way of reflecting the varying intentions of the evangelists in dealing with their material?

- In Matthew (10.5–15), Mark (6.7–13) and Luke (9.1–8) the disciples are given a commission to spread the good news. Is this account to be understood in the same way? If so what is the good news for the writer of this Gospel?

- Why do you think John has the risen Lord dissuading Mary Magdalene from touching him?

A Fishing Trip followed by Breakfast on the Beach

John 21.1–25

¹**Afterwards Jesus appeared again to his disciples**, by the Sea of Tiberias. It happened this way: ²Simon Peter, Thomas (called Didymus), Nathanael from Cana in Galilee, the sons of Zebedee, and two other disciples were together. ³'I'm going out to fish,' Simon Peter told them, and they said, 'We'll go with you.' So they went out and got into the boat, but that night they caught nothing.

⁴Early in the morning, Jesus stood on the shore, but the disciples did not realise that it was Jesus.

⁵He called out to them, 'Friends, haven't you any fish?'

'No,' they answered.

⁶He said, 'Throw your net on the right side of the boat and you will find some.' When they did, they were unable to haul the net in because of the large number of fish.

⁷Then the disciple whom Jesus loved said to Peter, 'It is the Lord!' As soon as Simon Peter heard him say, 'It is the Lord,' he wrapped his outer garment around him (for he had taken it off) and jumped into the water. ⁸The other disciples followed in the boat, towing the net full of fish, for they were not far from shore, about a hundred yards. ⁹When they landed, they saw a fire of burning coals there with fish on it, and some bread.

¹⁰Jesus said to them, 'Bring some of the fish you have just caught.'

¹¹Simon Peter climbed aboard and dragged the net ashore. It was full of large fish, 153, but even with so many the net was not torn. ¹²Jesus said to them, 'Come and have breakfast.' None of the disciples dared ask him, 'Who are you?' They knew it was the Lord. ¹³Jesus came, took the bread and gave it to them, and did the same with the fish.

¹⁴This was now the third time Jesus appeared to his disciples after he was raised from the dead.

¹⁵When they had finished eating, Jesus said to Simon Peter, 'Simon son of John, do you truly love me more than these?'

'Yes, Lord,' he said, 'you know that I love you.'

Jesus said, 'Feed my lambs.'

¹⁶Again Jesus said, 'Simon son of John, do you truly love me?'

He answered, 'Yes, Lord, you know that I love you.'

Jesus said, 'Take care of my sheep.'

¹⁷The third time he said to him, 'Simon son of John, do you love me?' Peter was hurt because Jesus asked him the third time, 'Do you love me?'

He said, 'Lord, you know all things; you know that I love you.'

Jesus said, 'Feed my sheep. ¹⁸I tell you the

truth, when you were younger you dressed yourself and went where you wanted; but when you are old you will stretch out your hands, and someone else will dress you and lead you where you do not want to go.' [19]Jesus said this to indicate the kind of death by which Peter would glorify God. Then he said to him, 'Follow me.'

[20]Peter turned and saw that the disciple whom Jesus loved was following them. (This was the one who had leaned back against Jesus at the supper and had said, 'Lord, who is going to betray you?') [21]When Peter saw him, he asked, 'Lord, what about him?'

[22]Jesus answered, 'If I want him to remain alive until I return, what is that to you? You must follow me.' [23]Because of this, the rumour spread among the brothers that this disciple would not die. But Jesus did not say that he would not die; he only said, 'If I want him to remain alive until I return, what is that to you?' [24]This is the disciple who testifies to these things and who wrote them down. We know that his testimony is true.

[25]Jesus did many other things as well. If every one of them were written down, I suppose that even the whole world would not have room for the books that would be written.

This final chapter of John is thought by most scholars to have been added as an afterthought, possibly by another hand. The author is certainly 'in tune' with the style of the rest of the Gospel and reflects John's theology by making a number of allusions to other parts of the Gospel. The main purpose of this chapter is to provide some clarification about Peter, whose understanding of the resurrection is not clear and whose reinstatement with Jesus needs to be dealt with. The previous chapter had emphasized the commission to the disciples to forgive or retain sins. Peter, having denied Jesus, is an obvious candidate for this sort of treatment. Most of the main disciples we have met in the last chapter are here, with the addition of Nathanael. They are engaged in an abortive fishing trip in the sea of Tiberias. Exactly what they are doing fishing when they have been commissioned as apostles is not explained. Perhaps we are to conclude that Peter has returned to his old profession and the others have been persuaded to join him in the hope of lifting him out of his depression.

Whatever the reason, the trip seems to be going badly. They have toiled all night and caught nothing – not an easy thing to achieve in a lake which is usually teeming with fish. We can only speculate on Peter's mood. He is no good at being a disciple and not much better at being a fisherman. It was at a similar low point, at daybreak, when Mary Magdalene met Jesus in the garden. Now, at first light, Jesus calls to the disciples from the shore. Again, we have the same pattern. At first the disciples do not recognize Jesus. Then, after a familiar sign or action, the recognition takes place. The beloved disciple, who was the first to come to faith without the evidence of hard proof, is again the first to recognize Jesus at a distance and says, 'It is the Lord' (v. 7). This is the cue for Peter to get dressed and dive overboard and swim ashore. Instead of a reprimand, Peter and the others are addressed affectionately as 'children' (v. 5), a term we meet with in the letters of John. This may be seen as something that encouraged Peter to approach Jesus. There are a number of allusions to previous Galilean experiences, including the miraculous catch of fish recorded in Luke 5. The main links with the rest of the Gospel are with the feeding miracle in John 6, and the charcoal fire in the courtyard where Peter made his threefold denial (18.18).

The scene ends with Jesus questioning Peter's loyalty three times and his contrite response. This an obvious allusion to the threefold denial. The commission to feed the sheep and the lambs is a reference to the image John has already presented of Jesus as the 'good shepherd' in chapter 10. Peter's behaviour in denying Jesus was more like that of a hired hand who deserts the sheep in times of danger. He has to be taught a lesson about his priorities if he is to have oversight of the flock and be a driving force in the mission of the new community alluded to in the catch of fish. We are told that he was hurt by these repeated questions. By re-enacting his shame, Peter is, in the words of John Wesley's hymn, 'ransomed, healed, restored, forgiven'.

Peter is reinstated and has felt the pain and remorse referred to in the other Gospels when recounting the denials. He is instructed to 'follow' Jesus (v. 19) the 'good shepherd', who laid down his life for the sheep. Peter as under-shepherd must look ahead even to martyrdom if necessary. When Peter enquires after the beloved disciple's fate he is told not to worry on that score (v. 22). The writer then uses this as an opportunity to disclaim any rumour that the beloved disciple will live forever. Some take this to be further evidence to link the beloved disciple's identity with that of Lazarus, whose possible immortality might have been the source of speculation because he had been raised from the dead by Jesus. The text ends by claiming that the authorship of 'these things' is by that same disciple. In other words, the content of this chapter and the rest of the Gospel is derived from the writings and reflections of the beloved disciple.

The final verse of the Gospel refers to the endlessly rich seam of stories about Jesus. The writer concludes by reminding us that he (like the other Gospel writers) has made a very careful selection. The reason for this selection has already been given at the end of the previous chapter. It was also given in the opening verses of the Gospel; those who receive the Jesus presented in these pages 'who believe in his name, are given power to become children of God' (1.12). It has to be said that the mysterious unnamed 'beloved disciple' displays all the characteristics of the ideal follower of Jesus. He provides the reader with the perfect model for discipleship as one who is close enough to lay in the bosom of the Son, as the Son is known to lay in the bosom of the Father (1.18). To understand discipleship in these terms is to open the heavenly door to an abiding relationship with the Father through the Son. This Gospel might begin in the heavenly sphere with the pre-existent 'Word', but it certainly ends on firm ground, with ordinary men and women having their eyes opened to the divine splendour which God has made known to those willing to see.

- In which ways is the purpose of this Gospel different from that of the other Gospels?

- How do you respond to the character of Peter in John's Gospel?

- Who do you think wrote this Gospel? Is it more important to know who wrote it or why it was written?

- Given the opportunity, would you have written this final chapter differently?

Interviews

Mary Magdalene

Misunderstood but determined to follow Jesus to the grave, only to find that she is the first witness to the resurrection and the one to carry the good news to the disciples.

me: How does it feel to be treated as the *femme fatale* of the Gospel story?

M: I'm used to it. Men need to give women some kind of image. It's the only way they can handle us – part of the process whereby we are dehumanized as the 'blonde bimbo', or in my case the 'fiery redhead'.

me: It's fascinating to trace your treatment by artists down the ages. You are either shrieking at the foot of the cross, clutching in the garden or howling in the desert. Do you think John is responsible for any of this?

M: No, not really. There is a certain confusion in the Gospels about my identity. Having been labelled a prostitute from the earliest times, I am usually identified with the 'woman who had led a sinful life' who anointed the feet of Jesus in Simon the Pharisee's house in Luke (7.37). I have to remind you that there is no justification for this in the text. The story is told in several forms in all four Gospels, and nowhere is it stated that Mary Magdalene is a prostitute.

me: You sound as if you resent this.

M: Not entirely. It is the only way some men can cope. Part of the problem is the number of Marys in the Gospels. Almost every woman is called Mary. There are at least five of us. It's as if you are not a man you must be called Mary. If you are not the Virgin then you must be a whore. So most of the other women named Mary or otherwise become me. I'm surprised that I'm not thought to be the woman at the well; we seem to share a similar reputation.

me: Do you see yourself as some kind of representative woman?

M: Whether I see myself as that or not, that's the way many see me.

me: Your role in John hinges on this business of 'seeing' and 'believing'.

M: How perceptive of you! I appear twice in John's Gospel, once at Bethany, when I rather upset Judas by swamping Jesus' feet with some expensive 'aromatherapy', and then again in the garden on Easter Sunday.

me: So you are the sister of Martha and Lazarus?

M: Yes.

me: How did you get to be called 'Mary of Magdala'?

M: Well, I married young to a boy from that Galilean town. He used to sell us fish in Bethany. We fell in love and he took me up north. Soon afterwards he was killed in a brawl with a Roman soldier. As there were no children and it was dangerous to stay there as an unprotected widow, I returned home and lived with my younger sister and brother, Martha and Lazarus.

me: How did you come to know Jesus?

M: Well, I had heard him preach in Galilee and offered him lodgings when he came to Jerusalem. Bethany is only a few miles out of the city. Jesus felt really at home with us. It was a place where he could relax. He and Lazarus were like brothers. You may have noticed that some have thought him to be the role model for what John calls the 'beloved disciple'. It was certainly possible for Lazarus to have gained Peter access into the courtyard of the high priest. We were well known to the servants there.

me: So you were all together when Jesus came to supper that last time?

M: Yes. We were both witnesses of the last great sign that Jesus performed before the resurrection when he raised Lazarus from the dead. I had a lot to be thankful for, and it was then that I realized that this sign was a pointer to something else. All three of us were beginning to see Jesus in a new light. He told me then to keep the oils for the day of his burial. It was a time of great anxiety as well as rejoicing. We knew that the authorities saw him as a threat, and that business about raising my brother from the dead didn't help things. We were all in a certain amount of danger.

me: Tell me what happened in the garden that first Easter Day.

M: I can tell you what happened. The story is very well known. What John does in telling my story is to show you what is really going on: how the Word really becomes flesh in the understanding of his disciples and how they see and believe the 'glory as of the One and only, who came from the Father, full of grace and truth' (1.14).

me: That all sounds rather theological.

M: 'For a woman', were you going to say? It seems to me that most of the theological discussions in John's Gospel are with women. But enough of that. We must avoid stereotypes. That is also part of the resurrection message.

me: What is the resurrection message for you?

M: As your poet Robert Browning says, it is about seeing 'points' as 'stars'. Or as George Herbert has it, looking beyond the pane of glass and espying heaven. You British are better at poetry than theology.

me: I'm sure that you are correct. But wouldn't you say there was a certain poetic licence in John's Gospel?

M: Jesus appeared at the beginning inviting people to 'come and see'. He promised them an open heaven, direct access to the Father if they would believe in him. John puts that clearly and imaginatively. You can call that poetry if it helps.

me: What does 'believing in him' mean?

M: Seeing beyond him to the presence of God.

me: How did that happen for you?

M: When he called me by name. You see I had come to the tomb early to fulfil that commission that I had been given at the supper party – that of anointing him. When I found the temporary tomb empty I thought that the disciples had taken away the body to a more permanent resting place. But it was obvious that Peter and the 'beloved disciple' knew nothing. The story is well known – how they ran ahead, one peeping in, Peter bursting in, Peter 'seeing', the other 'believing' – even without much in the way of evidence. My turn to seek and to find came when I was asked twice who I was seeking. Eventually, it dawned on me that he was not dead but risen. It was like gaining the gift of second sight. I was no longer like the poor, lost lovesick woman in the Song of Songs (3.1–3). I knew him to be my teacher, 'Rabboni'.

me: I noticed that you use the form usually reserved for God alone. Is there any significance in that?

M: Of course. There is nothing without significance in this Gospel. It is written with the sole purpose that those who read it might see and then see beyond to the open heaven in their midst. To quote your poet George Herbert again, 'Heaven in ordinarie, man well dressed.' We'll forgive him his political incorrectness.

The Beloved Disciple

The enigmatic author of this Gospel who represents the true follower of Jesus.

me: You have been very reluctant to be interviewed. Why?

BD: I would have thought that obvious. I have kept a cloak of anonymity for so long now that this sort of exposure is unwelcome.

me: Would you rather not be known at all?

BD: Anonymity has its advantages. It helps focus the spotlight in the right area.

me: And where is that?

BD: I hate to repeat myself, but I had hoped that was obvious.

me: You sound as enigmatic as the Jesus of this Gospel.

BD: Perhaps we would both prefer it if you were to reach your own conclusions on the evidence that is presented.

me: Are you Lazarus or John the son of Zebedee?

BD: Does it really matter who I am? Isn't it more important to recognize who it is I represent?

me: If you say so. What or who do you represent then?

BD: If I were to tell you that I am the role model for true discipleship you would know no more than what the term 'beloved disciple' expresses.

me: Are you saying the beloved disciple is the one who best understands Jesus?

BD: The beloved disciple is one who responds to the Gospel. He or she who has heard the call to come out of the darkness of death. He or she who has his or her eyes opened. The one who recognizes Jesus to be 'the resurrection and the life'.

me: Is that the reason for writing this Gospel?

BD: The reason for the writing of this Gospel is that you may see and 'believe that Jesus is the Christ, the Son of God, and that by believing you might have life in his name'.

me: And what is 'life'?

BD: Something you have had breathed into you and something that you should enjoy in all its fullness.